Mending Scotland

essays in economic regionalism

Christopher Harvie

© Christopher Harvie 2004

First Published 2004
Argyll Publishing
Glendaruel
Argyll PA22 3AE
Scotland
www.argyllpublishing.com

British Library Cataloguing-in-Publication Data.
A catalogue record for this book is available from the British Library.

ISBN 1 902831 74 8

Origination Cordfall Ltd, Glasgow
Printing & Binding Bell & Bain Ltd, Glasgow

'A Polite and Commercial People'

In the eighteenth century sense politeness cropped up
between 'politics' and 'courtesy': something like Adam
Smith's 'sympathy': in other words, purposive
communication which maintained civility. Quite different
from the 'in your face' style of much contemporary
business and intellectual behaviour. Something always
cited in favour of Tony Blair was his charm and
consideration, in contrast to, say, Rupert Murdoch or
Gordon Ramsay. It's not a notable Scottish quality these
days: promises broken without explanation, deadlines not
met, promised payments not made, letters not replied to;
all of these are rather more likely to be encountered in
Scotland than in London or in Germany. There are
compensations in greater directness and more of a
community spirit, but our 'branch-plant capitalism'
probably adds mental inhibition to our relatively insecure
society, and doesn't help its further development.

Contents

Preface

To Carol Craig, Patrick Small, Pat Kane, Gerry Hassan, Tom Nairn, Mike Russell, George Kerevan, Wendy Alexander, Paddy Bort:

At various times in the last few months the economic condition of Scotland has intruded itself into our conversations or correspondence. At Tübingen I have also taken over the supervision of seventy or so lively students of 'Economics and Regional Studies'. The dialogue thus generated struck me as valuable both in terms of ideas and in the teaching techniques it enabled me to practice. It also coincides with two publishing deadlines: the much-revised fourth edition for Routledge of my *Scotland and Nationalism*, first published in 1977, and the completion of *North Britain: West Britain, 1860-1920* for Oxford, which featured Scotland at the top of its industrial tide.

I needed a succinct text for my students which could sketch the scope of regional socio-economic studies, and I also wanted to transmit the ideas and techniques generated through Scotland's industrial experience which seemed relevant to her present development problems. Yes, we have the wonders of e-mail and the web, and Tübingen Landeskunde is present on www.intelligent-mr-toad.de (see below), but the book, pocket-size, to be read in the bus, plane or train, still can't be beat, and Scottish publishing has continually come up trumps, native nous and skill producing a competitive and attractive article without the huge editorial/PR top-hamper of the metropolitan mega-concerns. Thank you Derek Rodger.

The attainment of Scottish autonomy was the work of Edmund Burke's 'little platoons', and its spirit will stay that way – the Holyrood saga will ensure that! – *Mending Scotland*'s 'sage advices' are meant to be practical, about getting a society to cohere and cooperate, and ought to be relevant across the political spectrum and our seven ages. There are after the Introduction and a concise Database, sections dealing with Economy, Media, Europe and Strategy. The book's roots are in the Scottish 'common-sense' tradition, from Adam Smith through Patrick Geddes to Walter Elliot and Tom Johnston, coupled with a practical appraisal of circumstances – the old Boer guerilla John Buchan encountered who in a tight spot said 'I will make a plan' – and a scepticism about big being best.

I sometimes refer to the last as 'the Swordfish strategy', after a story an old airman told at an Open University Summer School. He was in the hunt for the *Bismarck* in 1942, and his squadron on the *Ark Royal* was composed of ancient Swordfish torpedo planes, which could on a good day manage 80 mph. Attacking the formidably-armed battleship, they found the flak always burst ahead of them. The *Bismarck*'s pom-pom guns were programmed to log on to, and blow out of the sky, modern torpedo planes doing 120 mph. When the Swordfish crews discovered that, they knew they could go in close and low. One of their torpedos hit the *Bismarck*'s steering and the ship was doomed. Rough-and-ready equipment, quick thinking and brave men enabled to a victory which – though at terrible cost – contributed to the pacific, regional Europe in which we teach and learn.

Tübingen, 13 April, 2004

Basic– Facts
Gross Domestic Product in $ billion
(2004 estimates: source CIA)

	World	Germany	BaWü	Britain	Scotland
	51,410	2,270	340	1,660	132

Population in millions

	World	Germany	BaWü	Britain	Scotland
	6,379	82.4	10.7	60.3	5,0

Virtual Harvie   or   www.intelligent-mr-toad.de

You can follow up the subject matter of *Mending Scotland*
by accessing my website. There you will find, under
Mending Scotland sources and further articles listed under
Mending Scotland's chpaters: for example v.ii.RLEE means
review of Clive Lee *The Scottish Economy*.

ACOLLEY means article on Linda Colley in the *Times
Literary Supplement*

These will lead you to other reviews and articles that I've
written which are relevant to the subject of the chapter.
Simply access the website, click on Professor Harvie and
then click on Articles [A] or Reviews [R]. As for books or
very long articles that can't be squeezed into the website?
You'll find details of these in Professor Harvie: long CV.
Where these exist on disc, an e-mail can bring material
per attachment (within reason: a man must live!). Copies
of out-of-print books and articles can be ordered at
whatever's the going rate plus postage – profits to the
Welsh Studies Centre.

So, like Dr Who's Tardis, *Mending Scotland* gets bigger
when you open the door.

Mending Scotland

I. Introduction:
i 'Scotland the no-very-weel'

'It's easy speakin,' he moaned, 'But I got a post-caird yestreen sayin' that the new Road Surveyor would be round the day. He'll come an' he'll no find me, or else he'll find me fou, and either way I'm a done man. I'll awa' back to my bed an say I'm no weel, but I doot that'll no help me, for they ken my kind o' no-weel-ness.'

Ecky the road-mender in John Buchan,
The Thirty-nine Steps (1915)

I 'Faur ye weel, ye bitches?' Not quite. . .
Centralised Britain is thriving, devolved Britain is not. Discuss. The optimism of the London press – at least of the Murdoch tabloids and broadsheets – seems relentless, an attitude echoed laconically by Chancellor Brown. Yet when he flies north to Dunfermline East, do his perceptions change? At Holyrood MSPs and the McConnell Executive face cumulative socio-economic crisis. Growth has been running at a third the UK level, and most sectors are in trouble. Agriculture and fisheries, which have kept the place going since Skara Brae, are gripped by the aftermath of foot and mouth, the hopeless economics of the family farm, the penalties of overfishing and fish-farmed pollution in the sealochs. Textiles? Dawson, once market leader, has its shares at 12p, and outsourcing by the likes of Marks and Sparks has cut its swathe. Tourism was in deep trouble even before 9/11, and www.visitscotland.com is a serial disaster.

Manufacturing has fallen 14 %, and exports 32% since 2000. The remaining heavy inustries depend on subsidy and, hit by the new technology recession, Silicon Glen faces the Cyberclearances before its second-generation firms are out of their incubators.

Service-industry capitalism – a frog which enjoyed only a brief career as a cash-cow – radiates gloom. Scottish Media Group, which ran the *Herald* and STV, is threatened with takeover. Thins and Smiths have gone, leaving Scottish bookselling to Anglo-America. Over-extension gone wrong has dented Scottish Power and Stagecoach. The once-booming finance sector (remember Edinburgh Fund Managers, Aberdeen Asset Management?) now boils down to the Royal Bank and Standard Life, the latter hit by equity collapse, losing staff, and about to demutualise; the fat-cat bosses of both are regarded by many of their clients with loathing. Biotechnology was savaged by a dead sheep. Call-centre Scotland? 55,000 jobs helped by welfare-to work, but if you blink you'll miss it. Transport and health stumble and wheeze: James Meek's devastating *Guardian* investigation showed how £10 billion was blown on the West Coast upgrade, by banking on a signalling system not just unproven but unconstructed: a decent rail system is retreating to the 2020s, if then, while up to a billion is blown on five pointless miles of motorway in Glasgow. Scotland's one bus factory faces closure because of fraud. The new Rosyth-Zeebrugge ferry seems to have made it, but only just, against haulage firms using East European drivers on minimal wages. Football, the war-horse of national identity, seems ready for the vet, if not the knackers. As for health, Scots tend to be sick and old. It costs a lot to die.

A touch of the Private Frasers? 'We're aa doomed, ah tell ye, doomed!' can be overdone, but even if allowances are made, Scotland isn't at all the smiley happy person Gordon Brown would like her to be. I don't say this out of nationalist conviction but as a social historian with the worn shoe-leather of the hack.

'He has sold his heart/To that old black art,/That's called the daily press.' I have been doing so for forty-two years. Periodically, my 'condition of Scotland' stuff has been found interesting enough to reprint, with respectable – even notorious results (thanks, Tommy Sheridan, for putting–*Deep-Fried Hillman Imp* up there with Noam Chomsky and Michael Moore) – and I get consulted by younger and more interesting politicians of all parties, and serve on more advisory committees and public bodies than I care to think of.

If Conor Cruise O'Brien can define an Irish writer as someone 'who has been mauled by the place' then my Scottish credentials will pass, though keeping out of the 'who-whom' business means I can write about ideas without having to compromise them for one deal or another: '*unbestechlich, aber käuflich*' as the Germans put it, 'Can't be bribed, can be bought.'

Tübingen Landeskunde is an eccentric but quite viable *Mittelstandsbetrieb*, whose dividend lies in the graduates it produces.Their attitude to Scotland is probably that of medical students being hauled round the wards by their prof. The condition of Scotland is on show, and the tone is dour – Carol Craig's *The Scottish Crisis of Confidence* (Big Thinking, 2003) Andrew O'Hagan's *The Death of British Farming* (LRB, 2001), Ian Jack's *The Crash that stopped Britain* (Granta, 2001), Tom Nairn's *Pariah* (Verso, 2001), Neal Ascherson's *Stone Voices* (Granta, 2002) – austere, if not mauling titles, every one. I have my reservations about psychological explanations of the national malaise, and O'Hagan seems too rejectionist about Ascherson's *Stone Voices*, though it hasn't the shattering impact of his *Black Sea*, which compares with his own fine reportage in *The Missing*; but the tone of many books about Scotland is retrospective, as if the book itself has become a place of refuge from a press and media obsessed with transitory celebrity.

Looming over all this is the much greater malaise of the 'matter of Britain', and in particular of the threat to journalism and open discussion. The *Economist* editor Bill Emmott's apologia for free market capitalism *20/21 Vision* (Penguin, 2002) proved a useful sparring-partner in writing this, Emmott quite justifiably regarding the journalist as a licensed paranoid, duty-bound to query every generalisation put about by the powers-that-be. More worrying was Professor Julia Hobsbawm, in the

Guardian, claiming that 85 % of journalists' stories depended on PR. Since Hobsbawm was the partner of Sarah Macaulay, wife of Chancellor Brown, this suggests a relationship which is simply too close. Scotland is already remote from British decision-making, and PR disproportionately reflects metropolitan opinion. In an economy increasingly dependent on high-value services, the generation of ideas has paramount importance; and if we have an information highway, we need to use it and not wait for the predigested stuff to be delivered to us.

So my central concern is with the sort of dialogue we need. Or what undergrowth has to be cut away before we see the state of the nation? For a few months after 1 May 1997 there was the sense throughout Britain that people were again speaking 'wi' the haill voice', and that we had a government prepared to listen and to assess priorities. Then the true dimensions of spin became apparent, not just in that first dodgy deal with Formula One, but in the rhetoric of initiatives, task forces, awareness campaigns, Tsars. In Scotland this showed up crudely, because our leaders weren't very good at it, and PR took the form of *tabloidistas*, simian limbs crammed into sharp suits, offering to rearrange the features of their critics. More serious is the sense that PR has become a self-propelling weapon, that 'hype' doesn't mean 'lies' as it did in its shady American past but a relentless, interchangeable selling of film stars, novels, life insurance, lifestyle, housing, politicians, restaurants, supermarkets, little different from junk post and spam mail.

Our 'condition of Scotland' books may be a sign of intellectual exile rather than the health of our media: a language which doesn't communicate outside a concerned minority. But the situation is serious enough to make *Mending Scotland* something more than a teaching unit.

II 'Tis Eighteen Years Since?'
Academics, particularly exile ones, are regarded as inhabiting ivory towers, but in 1969-80 (and most critically in 1969-71) I helped set up the Open University, one of the few success stories of modern Britain. In 1980 – mauled by the 1979 failure of

devolution – I moved to Germany and published a rather gloomy history of twentieth-century Scotland *No Gods and Precious Few Heroes* – now, with a slightly more upbeat tone, going into its fourth edition. In 1988 the BBC asked me to make a programme in their *Scotland 2000* series called 'Grasping the Thistle', and I made out the case for devolution by contrasting Scotland with the industrial dynamism of Baden-Württemberg. I argued that at the very least, German-style federalism would aid Scotland's recovery from being a problematic UK region; and that it might release springs of creativity, mutuality and enterprise which had been hemmed in by bureaucracy and remote government by a party, the Conservatives, which had an ever-diminishing foothold in Scottish life. This had some effect in energising the cause of Scottish autonomy.

It could also be seen as one of several moves towards a 'stakeholder society' of which Will Hutton's *The State We're In* (1993) was the most vivid example. Matters got far enough for Hutton and a big production-crew to descend on my Tübingen flat in October 1996 to film part of their *False Economy* series. Not only did the promised cheque fail to turn up, his stakeholder society proved even more elusive. From 1987, in fact, Scotland and Baden-Württemberg were going in quite different directions. Labour's one serious attempt at industrial modernisation, the manifesto of 1992, lost them the election and after John Smith's death in 1994 Tony Blair and Gordon Brown sacrificed manufacturing reconstruction to winning at all costs.

As a result the environmentalist basis of Baden-Württemberg regionalism has no Scottish parallel, despite the claims and projects of the new Parliament. There was no 'green' transport policy like that of the Stuttgart CDU/FDP government and its subordinate authorities, the *Communes* (towns) and *Kreise* (counties); the environmental goals, doggedly pursued in England by the non-Cabinet minister Michael Meacher, were scarcely paralleled. The result was that the manufacturing that could back up such policies was not revived, and skills and machinery steadily diminished. In 2004 the Scottish reputation in such matters as recycling, waste disposal and public health was awful, not just in European, but in world terms. On closer inspection, the link between this failure and the UK's apparent economic success was anything but coincidental. The country's enormous and growing enthusiasm for buying things seemed to have a direct link with its failure to get rid of them. While 50% of domestic rubbish in BaWü was recycled, in Scotland the whole shebang (oh, all right, 92%) was dumped in landfill sites: only one aspect of a series of economic dysfunctions and false rationalisations which had Scottish society in its grip. We had not just failed to improve our industry, we had actually developed a discourse about it which prevented us understanding it.

This gridlock – one of many – contrasts with the Holyrood Parliament's vast cost and limited powers. Single problems might be magicked away by the dividend on 'enterprise': the usual New Labour mantra. Ganging-up – imagine the above as a malign input-output table – they threaten to become insoluble. Holyrood has, for sure, turned in good research and policy reports, in fields neglected by the old bureaucratic régime, but new governmental systems require time to run themselves in. Conflicts over priorities, lack of skilled personnel, deficient social engineering, friction between new legislature and local authorities, threaten a chronic dysfunction, which will swallow the cash needed for innovation. As if this were not enough, a report from Prof Iain McLean of Oxford signals the end of Scotland's public finance being calculated by the Barnett Formula. Launched in 1978 with the bounty of North Sea oil looming, this stopped the Scots wanting to emulate Norway; its very favourable treatment bought the Union another couple of decades. The principle of regionalism in *England* will end it.

III An Accidental Economist

The direct genesis of this book was a reaction to the Fraser of Allander Institute's lectures on the future of Scotland in the winter of 2003-4: 'Magnificent Seven' suggested HG Wells's 'Samurai' of dynamic integrated social reform. Worrying enough. What we got were the sort of bland WASP males who had been handing out Nobel Economics prizes to one another for decades as a reward for finicky tweakings of the capitalist engine.

But its germ was actually planted by an incident near Inverness, when I was spirited away from a conference to speak to members of the local development authority. I had been hoping to talk to them about transport in Baden-Württemberg (the Black Forest has many similarities to the Highlands) and retailing alternatives to a big supermarket project which might be friendlier to tourism ('Come to Scotland and see the stunning malls' lacks something.) But a grandee from a multinational had turned up so we got wined and dined at a classy hotel. Much appreciated, but the bill would have paid twice over for my trip from Germany, or got me three months' work by a research assistant. Was the big fish landed? I don't know.

Now it struck me in retrospect that, from the standpoint of orthodox economics (or at least the sort we've got used to), this meeting would be judged a success. It had brought custom to a local tourist facility in a bad year – for this was after 9/11 and the hotel seemed very empty. It had perhaps increased the prestige of the locals with the grandee, and might lead to future cooperation. But somehow I doubted it. The supermarket development went ahead and has doubtless been acclaimed as a major job creator.

This coincided with work that one of my students, Helmut Zaiser, was doing on economic theory in the intervals of working for the Fraunhofer Foundation, which explores the social context of innovation and technology. He compared the economic philosophy of AC Pigou, the founder of 'welfare economics' and tutor of JM Keynes, with that of John Ruskin, the art critic, who through his writings on society and economics, notably

Unto This Last (1861), fascinated JA Hobson (and through him, Lenin), Gandhi, Tolstoi and Patrick Geddes. Under welfare criteria, only immediate economic benefit could be accepted as criteria for evaluating an economic transaction. By these, the Culloden meeting would be judged – like the Inverness supermarket – to have a positive outcome. By Ruskin's criteria, which assessed long-term impact on the 'life-chances' of those involved, the outcome was quite negative. Pigou's was the more respectable academic reputation, but over the previous century Ruskin had in fact affected humanity more, and seemed more relevant to our current situation.

As someone who is still teaching and enjoying it when most of my contemporaries have settled for early retirement, I found myself thankful for the old humanistic first year of the Scottish universities, valuing greatly the pol. econ. and moral phil. I learned from the likes of AJ Youngson and Thomas L Johnston, when it came to teaching young economists in Tübingen. The German seminar system, when it works well, also means that the students can instruct the teacher as well as the other way about, as with Zaiser: only one of many insights which my students brought in a process which taught me about PowerPoint while making me return conceptually to the roots of economics in the Scottish eighteenth century. Which is why I dedicate this little book to them.

A humanist economics is about determining the personality as much as the safety of the state. A key discovery of the Scots *literati* was the law of unanticipated consequences, that one transaction inevitably influenced all the others – an insight almost certainly transmitted to the theories of energy formulated by their contemporaries and formally articulated in the nineteenth century by another Scots polymath, James Clerk Maxwell in his Second Law of Thermodynamics.

Yet economics, as in Adam Smith's own career, is rhetoric (we would now call this 'spin'), as well as system. We determine the health of the body politic by assessing its inputs and outputs; its operation as a system and its impact on its individual actors, but rational self-regard and self-projection are also paramount

– 'O' wad some Pow'r the giftie gie us/Tae see oorsels as ithers see us' is Burns paraphrasing Smith. Economic equilibrium would always be a receding goal; society was kept together by a vision of its limits (the 'nation' or *polis* whose wealth was being created) and the sympathy, the sense of solidarity and trust, which held it together in its daily transactions.

But this humanist business was also accompanied in Adam Smith (and Burns: read 'The Twa Dogs' – has anything changed?) by a real sense of evil-doing; of social menace, of 'luxury and corruption' overthrowing the *polis*. My worry (inspired by incidents like the foregoing), was that if our economy ceased to be an enterprise with tangible and beneficial social goals, luxury and corruption would in fact take over. The goal of growth expressed in crude percentages might be sacrosanct, but (if it was there at all) it didn't seem to increase the long-term welfare of the country and its inhabitants.

In my efforts at self-education, I turned to the orthodox authorities of the economics profession – *Economica*, *The Economic Journal*, etc. – and returned increasingly dissatisfied. What seemed in fact to sustain my students and their often rather conservative teachers wasn't this fine-wrought costume jewelry but the existence of the powerful manufacturing-based engine of the Baden-Württemberg economy (33% in 2002, against 20% in Scotland), and the sense that everyone knew pretty well how it held itself and its society together. How could such people function in an economy like that of Scotland, where cause and effect were not at all straightforward? And where it was increasingly difficult to make long-term assessments?

IV Local Habitations
Two decades spent teaching and researching in Tübingen (where one of the Scots enlightenment classics *An Inquiry into the Principles of Political Oeconomy* (1767) was written by the exiled Jacobite Sir James Steuart, has also concentrated my attention on where economics shades off into theology or sociology or philosophy – as indeed it must have done for the eighteenth century *literati*. It hasn't changed all that much: the Neckar-

Athens still earns its keep. It is fashionable to mock German academia, but to be able to hear and meet the likes of Hans Küng, Ralf Dahrendorf, Mary Robinson, Marion Dönhoff and Joseph Lee would not have happened in a normal UK university.

Such encounters highlight in Küng's terms the 'global ethic' which surrounds economic decision-making. They also, in a symbolic way, focus attention on the means used to express economic identity. Take, for example, model railways. There are eleven million of these in Germany, probably one in every third family, and they keep a huge industry going in nearby Göppingen with its Märklin works and its 2000 engineers. (Britain's Hornby trains are of course built in China). The railway layout seems to be the *kleine heile Welt* – the small, healthy world – of the German *bourgeois*. It's not a control fantasy, or sexual substitute, so much as a symbolic picture of a society, helpfully miniaturised, where all aspects of life can be seen coming together.

This symbolism appeared in one of the more troubling books from modern Scots literature, Alan Warner's *Morvern Callar* (1996), a novel set in the rock-pool of receding Scottish industrial society. Morvern's boyfriend commits suicide, leaving a huge detailed model railway layout of Oban in the loft of the house they share. God in other words has cleared off and Morvern has to find herself, which after lots of bad sex and bad trips she seems to do in a combination of ritual dancing, self-communion, and motherhood, returning (like all those folk in Linklater and Gunn) to where she started out. In this way lots of Scotland's pre-industrial impulses get an airing but the industrial god, in whom they all hung together, has cut his throat.

When you turn from imaginative literature to the business pages of the *Herald* or the *Scotsman*, read in a chronological sequence from the 1970s on, you get a cognate image of disarticulation, of sporadic, unconnected stories of enterprises rising, falling, being taken over; but no sense any longer of a political economy of calculable life chances, or of a system which could be thus analysed. Rolled up in my office is the Scottish Council's elaborate *Input-Output Table of the Scottish Economy* of

1977, recording the transactions between sectors of the country at the beginning of the North Sea oil boom. It's almost like a German model train layout in its precision, but nothing like this would be possible today.

The result is that our vision of economic and social inter-connectedness is muddy and opaque. with even the Executive's GDP statistics (which in early 2004 revalued annual growth upwards by 75%) described by Fraser of Allander Institute as 'sheer blarney'. An equally disconcerting fog has settled over UK statistics and thanks to the Eurostat scandal, those of the EU, which means that in our 'information society', much of our information either can't be trusted or has been privatised.

What I'm trying to do in this book is to suggest how these various components can be rearticulated, not to rebuild the old 'workshop of the world', for that would now be impossible and undesirable – service industries are the engines of redistribution after all – but to work out the right sort of questions to ask, if our society is to be moulded to conserve and develop resources, strengthen the life-chances of all parts, and promote Patrick Geddes' helpful triad of *Sympathy: Synopsis: Synergy* – outcomes which are more than the sum of inputs. What's on offer here isn't original. It suggests rediscovering the social thought that the country has generated over several generations. Its subject is the stages of our own life and environment, the getting of wisdom, of partners, of children, the governance and protection of the community, the care of the weak and the old; the ultimate reckoning with age and death.

Smith, Steuart, Ferguson were part of a dialogue that also involved Burns, Scott and Carlyle. A similar nexus found itself in the 'paleotechnic' period – liberating carbon-powered industry but not controlling it – involving the physicists Clerk Maxwell and Kelvin, the sociologists Robertson Smith, JG Frazer and Geddes himself, in dialogue with the likes of Hugh MacDiarmid, John Buchan, Naomi Mitchison, James Bowie, Robert Grieve, Walter Elliot. The roots, at least, of a third dialogue are visible in our post-1979 intellectual life, equally powerful, but rendered, for the moment, less coherent because of our fractured economic *polis* and a Parliament which still has to bed itself in. But they exist.

V Shopping and Dropping

The analysis of Scotland's economic malaise is often confusing, not to say flatly contradictory. Too much activity in the service sector? Too much in the public service sector? Too much in export manufacture? At one level there's been phenomenal socio-economic resilience, moving from the heavy industries in their prime (1850-1920) to slump; to boom again (1935-1959). Then on to consumer goods manufacture, the incredible feat of North Sea oil, hi-tech manufacturing in Silicon Glen, high-value added services in Charlotte Square. At another we can see chances continually missed, and the gradual entropy of that resilience. The ultimate paradox is to have an economy directed by a dour and rational son of the manse which is either a European success story, or the devastation of our seed-corn.

In Germany, and particularly in Baden-Württemberg, the economy *is* pervaded by Broon-like prudence. '*Schaffa, schaffa, Häusle bauen*' – work, save, build – being the watchwords. In slump, this intensifies: Germans shop less, repair more, holiday at home. But in Britain recovery has come through a spending spree bankrolled by soaring house prices. Housing in Germany is largely a social service. BaWü had 4.5 million households in 1995, rising to 4.8 million in 2002, an annual increase of 0.75% (In Scotland household increase has been running at 3.8% annually). With most people renting, prices have flatlined – my rent has risen by 10% since 1994. This is reflected in the actual shrinkage of the German retail sector in the slump.

By contrast Britons' rackety private lives, and a finite supply of housing and housing land (controlled by the builders), has driven prices up. That of an Edinburgh house trebled in 1997-2004. Tapping this through remortgages or loans has financed shopping, and through it urban reconstruction – Bull Rings, Merchant Cities, Harvey Nicks – reassuring till one sees the surrounding zone of 'To Let' signs. The rise in retailing in Scotland can be charted, and it is formidable. About £18.4

billion, up by over 30% in 1990-2001 and employing 230,000.

Retailing (£19 billion in 2002) is a quarter of our service sector: huge, varied in terms of entrepreneurship, badly charted and not altogether predictable. The Coops, for instance, the motor of Scottish working class independence, have collapsed in the traditional central belt homelands, due to the rise of such shopping malls as Braehead and the Forge and their penetration by the English 'big five'. Yet they have held on spiritedly in rural areas and small towns and seen off such competition. There are also huge variations in small-scale retailing. In London, this is an almost wholly ethnic-minority business. Of the 30 small retailers and repairers in a hundred-yard radius of Edinburgh's Nicholson Square practically half the non-pubs (and restaurants) are immigrant-run, and important for integration. Businesses in the schemes – the fortified 'wee shops' – tend to be run by locals who can pay the costs inflicted by vandalism and crime, and may be subject to protection rackets.

Retailing once fitted into a diffuse pattern of skills which bordered on manufacturing. In St Boswells in the 1950s Mr Mitchell the tailor was 'services' but since he made suits, he was manufacturing; the same went for the joiner, the stonemason, even Ballantynes at the big village store, who blended their own whisky. If we examine a typical high street now, selling has completely taken over. On-the-premises repairs are rare, and goods sent in for repair tend to come back with the remark that it would cost less to buy the thing new.

Hyper-retailing has obvious economies: no repairs means no need to spend money on training personnel for skilled work, no costs involved in sending damaged equipment and spare parts around the place. The price of the original plus a hefty interest-rate on the plastic plus warranty means the customer can perhaps get through two pieces of equipment before he or she starts seriously to eat into profits. This means a complete dependence on importing, and slender profit margins, which might get thinner yet if customers start systematically playing the replacement game, or transport or warehousing costs increase sharply. Hence the bankruptcy of MediaWorld, which carried with it all the firm's warranties, or the problems of Dixons, faced with closing up to a third of its stores.

Retailing *looks* customer-friendly, but behind the façade, someone is being looted, some social costs are not being met. The replacement CD player will have been made in a Chinese sweatshop, and shifted by air or bulk carrier, or road – all forms of transport which pay only a fraction of their global costs. And as for risks, 0.6% of the containers at New York's terminal are inspected. The dud CD player will be dumped, where its toxic content will in due cause leak out into the water-table. As for the batteries to power the beasts. . . !

VI Addicted to Advice

In the 1980s an autonomous Scotland looked likely to contribute something quite distinctive to a crisis-ridden Britain, lodged in a torpid, over-bureaucratic Europe, with the sort of ideas being promoted in and around the Constitutional Convention, in the novels of Alasdair Gray, the political theory of Tom Nairn, and the development of a distinctive Scottish feminism. Can one say the same today? I fear not. The setback of 1979 meant that a generation born roughly between 1930 and 1950 passed two decades in political impotence, capable of making marginal improvements, but frustrated by the truly reactionary power of a timid establishment.

The result was that when the Parliament came into operation in 1999, most of the really original figures who had led the resistance to Thatcherism were actually over retirement age. O'Hagan's attack on Neal Ascherson's *Stone Voices* went wide of the mark, but if Ascherson couldn't get a seat in the Parliament that wasn't a plus for the civic nationality he championed. Dialogue with our new élite is rarely stimulating. Instead there's the replication of the metropolitan addiction to presentation over policy, and an obsession with (usually expensive) advice.

In 1963 McKinsey's undertook their first analysis of the BBC. In Broadcasting House they encountered the poet and Third Programme producer Louis MacNeice. 'Mr MacNeice', the man from McKinsey asked, 'in the last six months you seem to have produced no programmes. What have you been doing?'

'I have been thinking.'

MacNeice would not get away with that now. But his programmes are still as classic as his poems like 'Bagpipe Music', and where's Mr McKinsey? Maybe reincarnated in the Allander circus? Prof Edward Glaeser of Harvard came from this milieu. He had some sensible suggestions, notably the idea of a common strategy for the central belt, but then poured scorn on public transport improvements like trams and said 'the car is the future'. Maybe to be expected, as he came from the land of the $1 gallon, yet the American cities he lauded, like Boston, have excellent public transport, and he might have had the *nous* to realise that the Scottish Executive was already committed to it. So, as a net outcome, Glaeser seemed about as enlightening as Homer Simpson (cognoscenti of Springfield will recollect its abandoned monorail and unquestioning devotion to the automobile). Which raises a general question – perhaps inconvenient, but still important – about such advice: why is the USA regarded as the only possible instructor? There are many European regions – the 'Four Motors' of Baden-Württemberg, Catalunya, Rhone-Alpes and Lombardy, for a start – whose situations are similar to that of central Scotland, and whose development strategies (industrial, environmental, social) far more relevant.

A recent German scandal may yield further clues. The head of the *Arbeitsamt* or Labour Office (the equivalent of the Job-Centres) had to resign after admitting huge sums spent on advice from private firms, notably McKinsey and the German firm Berger. This led the press to detect a huge superstructure of advice of variable quality – often ludicrously inappropriate – united only in its huge cost. In Scotland dissatisfaction with Robert Crawford's management of Scottish Enterprise led to his replacement by Jack Perry. Crawford had come from Ernst and Young. His successor came from Ernst and Young. Our society, very weak in its technical and scientific discourse – the fates of oil-based research, bio-science, computer software, have all been gloomy – has a social science split between an underfunded academic sector and a prosperous commercialised one, concentrated in political and business consultancy and market research. The tendencies of all of these gravitate, as Will Hutton has written, like iron filings, towards the American magnet, and buttress a trans-national corporate and career structure in which Scotland recedes to a place in which to have conferences. This may have positive aspects, and I have dealt with these in III.iii, but it will always be shadowed by the instability of megabucks, proven with terrible logic in 9/11.

We all were moved to tears by the terrible fate of 'the poor young clerks who add/ the profits of the stinking cad' to quote that otherwise gentle soul John Betjeman. But I guess many of us could in the circumstances bear up, like Betjeman:

> And get that man with double chin
> Who'll always cheat and always win
> Who washes his repulsive skin
> In women's tears. . .

What we now know about CEO culture – the phone-number bonuses, the private jets, the pensions ring-fenced against their own incompetence, the trousering of stock options (up fourfold in the last decade) – doesn't ingratiate. It was an American Republican president, Theodore Roosevelt, after all, who coined the phrase 'malefactors of great wealth'. The American triumphalist postmodernists – Fukuyama and Puttnam – have stressed the importance of 'trust' as the glue of civil society, essentially a *réprise* of Adam Smith's 'sympathy'. Yet Smith, always leery about merchants advising us on morality, would have guffawed at the likes of Irwin Stelzer, confidant of both Rupert Murdoch and Gordon Brown, touting the virtues of neo-liberalism, while employed by Enron. . .

VII These be your scribes, O Israel!

In 1992, when the magazine *Radical Scotland* folded, there was the feeling that at least the broadsheets were taking themselves seriously as debating fora. And now. . . ? The tragi-farce of Scottish Media Group has seen the *Herald* pass to the American Gannet group, and the bean-counters seem to have moved in on what was some of the best and most experimental journalism in Britain. Alf Young, Murray Ritchie and Iain MacWhirter, 'students of politics' in the school of the late, great James Margach, have frequently been referred to in the course of writing *Mending Scotland*, but Pat Kane's E2 seems to have happened on a different planet.

The *Scotsman* – ah, the *Scotsman!* Time was when it had its finger on Charlotte Square's pulse and through the irreplaceable Frank Frazer, on the black stuff pouring out of the North Sea. Then the mysterious Barclay Brothers took over and installed Andrew Neil, who immediately sacked the excellent Brian Groom, founding-editor of *Scotland on Sunday*. Neil was a decent Tory journalist on the *Economist* – his long supplement on North Sea oil in 1973 was well-researched, largely opinion-free – then he was hired by Rupert Murdoch, given the *Sunday Times*, and discovered the magic of the PR handout: the first practitioner of the paid-for consumerism which makes most of every British broadsheet binnable. As a result, we have the Hootsmon.

'Woe, woe and thrice-woe!' Here comes the Prologue, without, alas, Frankie Howerd. Now I agree with Bill Jamieson that Scotland suffers from economic embolism – as James Cameron said of the demise of the *News Chronicle*; good circulation impeded by clots. Mostly he sees them in the state system, but makes an exception for the cloven-hoofed directors of Standard Life. As for his colleague, my article-commissioner and friend (not just in the MacDiarmidian sense) *ci-devant* Comrade Kerevan: moving from being a teenage Christian in an evangelical sect, to Trotskysim, then to Labour, then via the SNP – the *Scots Independent* still touchingly endorses his policy as 'independence' – to neo-liberalism of a Hayekian sort.

As a freelance with a day-job, I get by. But what disappears in all this is the press as a consistent debate on the sort of country we want to have: a doctor diagnosing the body politic. You get this in some of the letter-columns, and some – though only a minority – of the columnists: those prepared to substantiate arguments with research and factual comparison. But the consistent pursuit of an argument is rare, as are assessments of the health of potentially our strongest political force: the voluntary and mutual sector. We have a promising forum for the discussion of policy in the quarterly *Scottish Affairs* <www.scottishaffairs.org>, but how widely is it read? Prof Lindsay Paterson, its editor, admits he doesn't know. In a notable recent article Neal Ascherson surveyed the 'virtual Parliament' whereby, through the Web and Public Libraries, the public has access to Holyrood and can influence its proceedings. The facilities were remarkable, but the uptake disappointing.

This compares badly with the level of public discussion we are used to in Europe, where the local daily press (the papers that everyone reads) is of a high standard and policy issues are widely aired. In Scotland our mass-circulation tabloids the *Record* and the *Sun* fall far short even of Germany's notorious *Bild-Zeitung*, although the evenings raise the game a bit, and many tabloid journalists are, given the chance, as able as their broadsheet brethren.

Back to the mutual element: expanding in certain areas, contracting in others, changing in yet more. Environmental organisations, like the National Trust, have grown mightily in recent years, reaching 240,000 members in 2000. Churches and political organisations seem, despite their role in gaining autonomy, in steep membership decline, though their role may be changing, like that of the Scottish Trades Union Congress, from promoting a particular interest group to strengthening the mutual element in Scottish civil society. We all turn up in society playing various different roles – policy-maker, volunteer labourer, trade unionist, parent-teacher activist, leafletter, congregation member – some dominant, some subordinate, and in a healthy mutual sector these can balance out and empower.

Some social trends may only be temporary. Time spent in the home, and indeed in the country, declined in the 1990s with a sharp rise in mobility, tourism and (less encouraging) family instability. This seems likely to go the way of hyper-retailing, as some of our 'permanencies': the supermarket, the car, the cheap flight, are already matters of controversy. Our voluntary groups may be about to expand at last into the 'Civic Forum' area that the Constitutional Convention envisaged for them. If *Mending Scotland* can help in this, or goad activists into constructive indignation, not least with its author, it will have done its work. Could we generate our answer to *Die Zeit*, or *The Irish Times*? If only. . .

Confronted with 'I'm sorry, Professor Harvie, but we're being reorganised. . .' or Scotland the shelpit ('reorganisation' being the mechanism whereby at least Scotland's 20,000 surplus graduates are housed, often at the expense of the experienced and the competent) one sighs for John Stuart Mill's ideal of enlightened consumer haggling with competent producer, only to realise that this is as utopian as anything the left dreamed up.

'People of the same trade seldom meet together, even for merriment and diversion, but the conversation ends in a conspiracy against the public,' said auld Adam Smith. His answer to this was – in part – education. The answer of Rupert Murdoch, the most important Scot of our time, is ignorance.

ii The History we Need

I The History We Deserve?

> 'History to the defeated
> May say Alas
> But cannot help or pardon.'

Auden's lines are famous, but what does history say to the victors? A struggling movement – a class or a nation – must interrogate its failures or defeats, using this to rationalise, throw overboard old beliefs, reorganise. But a partially successful movement runs the risk of cashing-in its past. History got us here. We are its end. Enjoy.

We've heard such triumphalism from Francis Fukuyama and friends. Could the semi-success of Scottish self-government breed something similar: history no longer as process, but as something we can sell? Yes indeed.

The uptake of history in Scottish schools is disappointing. Assessments of this, notably by Sydney Wood, have shown islands of emotion – the 'Braveheart' factor – in a sea of ignorance. 50% of kids recognised Wallace, no-one recognised Tom Johnston. The new National Museum of Scotland gives the twentieth century over to a bring-and-buy sale where celebs and the public can exchange memories: Tony Blair's guitar, Kirsty Wark's Saab: a post-modern disaster, and – in a century of war, socialism, oil – a national disgrace.

If history is checked at the door, it will come slithering over the windowsill, in forms trivial and formidable. Not just sloppily-researched guides and souvenirs, the lightweight bookstalls in our culture centres that drove Rosemary Goring, the *Herald*'s literary editor, to tears, historical novels wide of the truth, but policies determined by emotion, not by analysis, like our obsession with rural land rather than urban poverty. Recent history ought to be the context for the policy of our infant state. But in sociology, literary criticism, politics and even social history, its enigmatic Cheshire cat grin registers confusion and stasis. Why?

II Parliament and Populism

Compare Ireland, which first suffered English *imperium* in the post-Union schools, then an equally dogmatic Irish Catholic nationalism. Post-1945 historians reacted to Ireland's neutrality with the 'revisionism' debate about Ireland's relation to European trends in economics, thought and culture. Professor Joe Lee is emotionally a de Valera republican but a meticulous European mind, who has done the state some service as Senator for Cork University. His *Ireland, 1912-1985* (Cambridge, 1990) arguably laid, in its careful and comparative critique of Irish politics' impact on society and economy, the foundations for the Celtic tiger-cage. This was the payoff of his experimental *Modernisation of Irish Society* (1973), the model for my own *No Gods and Precious Few Heroes* (1981), in which Lee stressed the centrality of intellectual history. But such realism is only fitfully present among our politicians, and may have got even more distant with self-government.

Present concerns select past facts. The Scottish Disruption – the split in the Kirk – of 1843 was boring in the 1960s, but not in the 1980s when the struggle for devolution questioned the parliamentary sovereignty against which the 'Non-Intrusionists' had in 1842 issued their 'Claim of Right'. This Calvinist title sanctioned the cross-party campaign, though the Chairman of the group which drafted it, Sir Robert Grieve, was a Catholic and Kenyon Wright, the ever-active fixer of the Constitutional

Convention, was originally a Methodist. This religious impact in a secular age didn't do anything to stop the once-great influence of the churches draining away. The Edinburgh parliament may open the way to rational enquiry and innovation – accessing a minister within hours, instead of a lengthy to-ing and fro-ing with London – but the Scottish political community has still to bed down (this took the regions from 1974-84). Into this vacuum facile ideology and populism can flow.

Britain suffers even more from its own anorexia, with a vague 'identity politics' replacing class or industrial politics. Much enthusiasm greeted Linda Colley's *Britons* (1992), whose 'imperial protestant' theme stressed religious and imperial unity over the 'mechanical' unity secured by industrialisation and transport change – though her evidence was patchy in Scotland, attenuated in Wales, and in Catholic Ireland non-existent. Norman Davies' *The Isles* (1999) expected that the UK would break up, but this bold coda came after a weakly anecdotal treatment of the nineteenth century. So was it surprising when Tom Devine's *The Scottish Nation* (1999), long on agriculture, demography and urbanisation (all important, sure), galloped through Victorian industrialisation in fifteen out of its 700 pages, and settled the cultural scene with a few strings of names?

III 'Scotland's Shame'

Another Devine volume showed more of a hangover: *Scotland's Shame* (2000). It was cued by a speech of the composer James MacMillan at the 1999 Edinburgh Book Festival. MacMillan wanted to emphasise the multiple nature of Scottish cultures, and the need to foster these. His targets were the prejudice of 'Old Firmism', often tacitly supported by the residues of the unionist establishment, a left-wing, anti-clerical threat to the Catholic school system established as part of the state network in 1918, and a philistinism that went back to the Reformers' destruction of music and ceremony, painting and stained glass in Scottish churches. Walter Scott, Edwin Muir and George Mackay Brown had said this long before. The problem was the way the issue ballooned into prominence. Various opinion formers reacted critically to MacMillan before reading his speech, so a pause for self-examination might have been in order. Instead the mills of publicity ground, and *Scotland's Shame: The Book* emerged.

After the deluge of devolution the waters had receded and the dreary stadia of Ibrox and Parkhead stood out again. But were any new questions being asked? Where did community loyalty stand when scarcely a single Scot played for Rangers? Where did the Tartan Army differ from the collective dementia of English laddism's 'beautiful game'? Or indeed from its world-wide 'industrialisation'? Were the yobs of Charleroi yelling 'No surrender to the IRA', borrowing direct from militant Ulster protestantism, linking it up with right-wing politics and the 'squaddie culture' of troops based in Northern Ireland? On all such topics there was silence.

One telling line came from Andrew O'Hagan, whose *Our Fathers* had rightly been nominated for the Booker, claiming that Catholics were invisible in the modern Scottish novel. Where had the lad been? If anything Catholics had dominated the genre from Patrick McGill via A.J. Cronin and Bruce Marshall to William McIlvanney. Did O'Hagan feel that he could get away with this in London literary circles? Probably: don't switch off the few northern lights the Groucho Club can make out.

The Catholic Church had good scholars in the *Innes Review* and elsewhere, those closest to it *were* interesting. Bishop Joseph Devine insisted on the 'embourgeoisement' of Scots Catholics. Tom Gallagher, with experience of right-wing Catholic nationalism in Portugal and ethnic tensions in the 'new' East Europe, related Glasgow's problems to these menacing backdrops. Devine's own contributions were as balanced and self-critical as MacMillan's.

But the *lacunae*! Only one woman in the book; nothing about theology or the actual content of education; nothing on our conservative hierarchy, our absent 'People's Church' (so distant from Holland, Germany and Austria): instead a near autistic sociology remote from historical roots or wider culture, a Scots-

Irish obsession, remote even from Ireland, whether Ulster, revisionism or the crisis in the Irish Church. Compare this with Ciaran Brady's *Interpreting Irish History* (1994), or McGonigle, O'Rourke and Whyte's sparky anthology of Scots-Irish writing *Across the Water* (2001).

No-one noticed that while Scots civic nationalism – covenants, claims of right, and so forth – echoed militant Calvinism, it hadn't damaged Catholic representation, but Scotland's other minorities were out of the loop. Their one success – the election of Mohammed Sarwar as Westminster MP for Govan – met with a public pillorying no Scots Catholic had ever suffered. As for the 'socially excluded' on troubled estates, they got represented at Holyrood by the douce Labour bourgeoisie of Kelvingrove and South Edinburgh. *Scotland's Shame* was aimed – like the guns of Singapore – away from the real combat. On gays, education and marriage – only weeks before Clause 28 was to convulse Scottish opinion, allying a near-medieval prelate, Cardinal Winning, with a puritan capitalist, Brian Soutar – it fell into complete silence.

IV Rivers of Loss

Sociology was alienated: the hope of 'progressive' academics in the 1960s, it had faded into providing recruits for privatised market research and consultancy, and was further squashed by the events of 1989-91. 'Scotland the Brand' seemed heavy irony to academics, but was taken wholly seriously by businessmen. Rather too many former far lefties became born-again capitalists, though this might be expected among the 'great impersonal forces' people: the locomotive of economic causality was simply running down another track.

Our PR élite were, however, tyros at making money, compared with the sleekit suits of Standard Life or the Royal Bank, or the Edinburgh professionals who pulled off the Holyrood heist. They had not politicised the discussion of oil, or manufacturing, or retailing, or recycling – or that huge 'fourth sector' of crime. By 2004 populism was squeezing the pimple of 'anti-social behaviour' (a wee Scottish version of Blair's quest for 'weapons of mass destruction') without troubling to investigate the toxic cultural diet which bred it.

There seemed among the intellectuals a waning faith in politics, and in history as their record. Cairns Craig had stage-managed the country's literary recovery in the 1980s. As one of the founders of *Cencrastus*, editor-in-chief of the *History of Scottish Literature* and the *Determinations* series run from Polygon, he helped shift cultural discourse away from the hurt of 1979 and made it think experimentally about past and future. But by *The Modern Scottish Novel* (1999) Craig had seemingly grown sceptical of historical continuity, and the unifying factors of the novels that he studied – from *The House of the Green Shutters* to *Trainspotting* – became myth, linguistic or psychological conditioning. This meant a continuing circularity, without any possibility of progress. Where some scholars differentiated between regional poetics and MacDiarmid's aim of 'seeing Scotland whole', Craig was re-erecting a centre-point, but one reduced to the cultural paralysis of the birds in James Kelman's wilderness.

Parallel to Craig, yet in some ways as perplexed, was the great guerilla himself: Tom Nairn's *After Britain* (1999) had a brilliant critique of a New Labour deluding itself that, despite devolution, parliamentary sovereignty yet lived. But Nairn gave Scotland an uncharacteristic pathos, and his enthusiasm for Colley's *Britons* was ironically shared by Blair and Brown. He saw a continuing 'wound' to Scottish identity, inflicted by the Union, 'a hidden river of loss', against which civics wasn't gutsy enough.

This line had been put over in *Subverting Scottish History* (1993) an eloquent assault on eighteenth-century 'improvement' by Colin Kidd from that redoubt of ancient Britishness, All Souls, mourning the destruction of traditional Scottish history by rationalist London-oriented Whigs; Edwin Muir's 'shallow banishment' of the people from their history echoed hollowly from somewhere close to the River of Loss.

V 'Luxury and Corruption'

What ought to have been here was an economic and social history of post-1980. John Foster and Charles Woolfson had done wonders on shipbuilding, heavy engineering and oil, Keith Aitken on the STUC, but for the rest – hi-tech manufacturing, finance, transport and retailing – it was back to the press cuttings.

To unearth a radical of the Enlightenment like Thomas Reid, was however to encounter Scottish ways of thought and local *virtù,* but with king-lists, chronicles or ballads, and the dynamism of a politics which was not just civic but technological and scientistic. These ideas had pursued Adam Smith's 'sympathy', migrated to urban, social, religious or educational discourse, and often physically moved overseas. This was not much evident in Devine's long but repetitive *Scotland's Empire* (2003). In *The Scottish Nation* industrial economics tended, along with the Promethean Scots *bourgeoisie,* one of Europe's most powerful, to be sidelined, while Devine back-projected the dominant Labour particularism. But in a fold of the landscape old monsters and fierce debates still lie concealed.

Paid-for history didn't want to be reminded of the industrial past – triumphs as well as decline. Its preferred image was 'Scotland-the-Brand' as a financial control-room cum rest-and-recreation centre: a mirage which has thrived as the market has gone hyperactive and the industrial machinery itself has slowed down and seized up. Or in Rupert Murdoch's hitherto unerring appreciation of Anglophone humanity's lines of least mental and moral resistance, has the fabrication of money-myth become a Scots' leading edge – whether it's Harry Potter and Edinburgh as the Golconda of wonderful literary success, the chemical hedonism of Irvine Welsh, or the 'gold-leaf binding' of millionaire golf or whisky trails? Are we in what Adam Smith and Adam Ferguson would have called 'luxury and corruption' country, when Locate in Scotland could assure German industrialists that wages and professional salaries in Scotland were 'satisfactorily low'? Scotland's gains from 'disorganised capitalism' may partly be negated by the immediate reality of a third living in poverty, manufacturing gripped by the high pound, crisis in farms and fishing, but if coping with this keeps Holyrood's role minimalist, who in London is going to worry about that?

History would at least suggest that these be explored as our equivalents to the social alienation and wretched living conditions that Victorian Scotland failed to cope with, and which brought it down after 1918. Solidarity may be only a luxury to the bodyguard-capitalism of an Ayn Randy American élite. We have to construct it, and this time in a situation where the longer-term implications of hyper-marketism are dark: definitive social breakdown and climate catastrophe. We misread the record at our peril, and without the chance of a second attempt.

II. Economics
i. People Politics

Friends: Remember that Scottish population is conveniently bang on 5 million; calculate the Scottish proportion of most British statistics by multiplying by 8.3%. This will pretty quickly show whether a Scottish statistic is predictable or quite out of order (like drugs).

I Babies

Scotland, Sweden and Baden-Württemberg started the twentieth century with similar populations of about 4 million. In 2000 Sweden was 8.8 and Ba-Wü had risen to 10.5 million, Scotland had crept timidly up to 5 million, and was slipping back. A small population in a western industrial country ought to suggest high output per capita: not so. Ba-Wü managed $29.4k, Sweden $27k, Scotland a pretty ordinary $23k.

Cue former Enterprise Minister Wendy Alexander, who not long after getting married in autumn 2003, opted enthusiastically for the promotion of motherhood, in particular for the notion that graduate women should give birth sooner rather than later, the *sotto voce* argument being that if they didn't, then those less fitted for motherhood would outbreed them. This was one of those New Labour think-tank ideas that went far beyond the right-wing notions of the late Sir Keith Joseph, which cost him the Tory leadership in the 1970s. As for proxy votes for parents of large families, which also cropped up in a *Demos* paper, this was a pet project of Archduke Otto von Habsburg, Catholic traditionalist, CSU MEP, and not exactly a beacon of the European left.

Are we recreating the matriarchy of early Celtic society? No bad thing. Among London's West Indians, black ladies dressed like the Queen Mum raise some of the capital's brightest kids – black teenage girls have an enviable record in A-levels – while rubbishing their feckless fathers. That you don't have to be black to be feckless is demonstrated in everyday Scottish life. As a member of the Majestics, John Byrne's notoriously dysfunctional rock band, said to Vince Diver, 'That wee girl didnae kill hersel because she lost her bairn. She kilt hersel because she found one – you!' Teenage motherhood may be less a mistake than a way out of a way out of a society dominated by dim men, a journey with an adoring companion who will draw assistance towards you from families which are otherwise weak. The problem will usually not be maternal incompetence, but the return of the immature male.

Tots in the household are one thing; tots exposed to the ravening maw of commercialism are quite another. Conservatives denigrated old socialist advocates of child-centred education like A.S. Neill and R.F. MacKenzie, but these were innocuous in comparison with the present day. Businesses specifically target kids' 'pester power', isolate individualist kids from their friends, and try to mould them as small but perfectly-formed (i.e. fat) consumers. Scots families, publishing and entertainment usually copes pretty well with the early years. At secondary school something quite different happens.

II Yoof

Given an ageing population, and the need to maintain it in its old age, we ought to be very encouraging about the younger generation as our potential saviours. Are we? Has youth ever been regarded quite so pessimistically? Not as the resources of hope but as omens of social despair. Own up, McConnell, when you needed a populist theme to pull you out of schtuck in the

May 2003 election, yoof came to hand (or was handed to you by David Blunkett) just in time for front-page treatment in the *Record*. 'Anti-social behaviour' was as elusive, statistically, as 'weapons of mass destruction', since the stats showed that minor, youth-based crimes were declining, and had anyway a far lower level than in England. Yet the gambit worked, at least up to a point, in the anomie-ridden, sink-scheme, society created by 'bent Scotland' (see section II.v).

The statistics of socialisation – basically training – weren't promising. About 25% of Scots kids left school without any qualifications (the Ba-Wü level was 9.1%) and although university uptake was broadly similar (30% Scots to 28% Ba-Wü, with the Scots taking half the time to get their degree!) the intermediate level of vocation qualification was poor, and hadn't improved for a decade. Typically, 'modern apprenticeships' saw only a third hitting their targets, and the less said about the Chancellor's billion wheeze of Individual Learning Accounts the better.

The result was a large minority of undercommitted and unengaged Yoof was seen as politically and socially apathetic, consumption-driven, at worst willing fashion victims, captivated by an international hip-hop culture which was basically that of criminals and pimps, coolly and callously marketed by American firms. I can't think of a single articulate defence of – or even attack on – them coming from their own generation. 'Thick was cool'. Everyone had their own stories to tell of baseball-capped, trainer-shod idiocy.

Logically, more affluent teenagers – with apparently about £200 million spending money, mobile and aware of new forms of information and self-expression – ought to be more fortunate. Yet they weren't. In the past 'boy wonder' Horace Broon used to power ahead on enthusiasm and energy. Yet an analysis of a week's stories in the *Edinburgh Evening News* showed, overall, apprehension, shyness, unease. Presenting awards in 1999 at an essay competition run by the late John Smith's Bookshops I found the winners were all from fee-paying schools. Yet even then their own outlook seemed pessimistic. Is this peculiar to

Britain? So it seems. Why? Is there a specific combination of family breakdown, individual isolation, commercial targeting, irresponsible sexualisation, declining articulacy and physical inertia which has brought this about? German research in the 1990s showed that far from kids ganging up, much of their play was quite lonely. Glued to a TV or VDU showing God knows what – shrieking teen hosts or the web's vast slough of porn – or Scotland's speciality of ultra-violent video games? If outside, kids were stuck to sound-systems or mobile phones which blocked out the aural and even the visual environment, just as the car had evicted them from the streets: the jostling and swearing – 'Hau ab!'/'Fuck off!' – wasn't rebellion but inarticulacy.

This generation has enjoyed political rights from eighteen since 1971 (a simultaneous, Europe-wide change never properly researched). Two generations earlier, the boys would be expected to fight for their countries. Yet the impression given in a recent *Herald* survey of teenage Scots was one of passivity, manipulation and lack of initiative, even among those – such as students – whose life chances should have been pretty good. To visit the *glacis* of megaboozers which surrounds our universities is sobering: not least for my German students, aghast at 'merry teenagers' drinking themselves silly at two in the afternoon. Key into an internet portal – for instance that of Wanadoo – and encounter an intellect-free zone. And don't look at the burgeoning lads or ladettes' mags with any hope of encountering originality, responsibility, conspicuous virtue or even intriguing vice.

Such statistics as we have shows that these problems can be encountered anywhere in Europe – the graffiti-count seems worse in Germany, Holland and Italy than in Britain. (My father, ever the dominie, said at least these kids worked hard at it: ours were just scribbling.) But in key areas of education and culture the figures are against us: the narrowest minds, the greatest alcohol use, the worst sexual health. A huge resource going to waste? Or in the case of unintegrated minority males, to something a great deal worse?

There is another element. If there is a youth problem, then

it ought to be articulated. Yet popular treatments of this – dominies with attitude: MacKenzies and Neills – seem few. Youth figures little in, for example, *Scottish Affairs*, in the conferences of the Centre for Scottish Public Policy, in books like Dave McCrone's *Understanding Scotland*. Beyond school visits, there's nothing for it in the Scottish Parliament, actual or virtual. Can blame for this be put on the teaching profession? For a fifty-nine year old, looking back, teachers were monumental figures, some dreadful but many inspiring. Yet after thirty years writing about Scottish social issues, being involved with German teacher training, and lecturing to teachers' groups throughout Europe, I can number approaches from Scottish teachers, training colleges and unions on the fingers of two hands. Has this class, once the conscience of the country – the motor of the centre-left – simply given up? Certainly the fiction, from George Friel's *Mr Albert MA* to James Kelman's *A Disaffection* suggests surrender, in the face of fearsome odds.

Economic exploitation gets us part of the way. In the 1950s the child was pretty well master of his or her choices: in and out of rather large families, which could look out for each other: then friends, sports of one sort or another, school societies, a plethora of church groups or film clubs, cubs, scouts, BBs, hobbies, reading, radio, TV. There was a skill in play: from peevers and conkers to football, bikes and fishing, leaving aside the empty roads and after about eight-years-old the general liberty to walk, cycle, or take the bus wherever. Now, one doesn't have to read Jeremy Rifkin on the privatisation of public space to register the restricted choices, the powerful images of infotainment and promotion, which impact with full force on the adolescent. He or she is both more dependent (particularly on parents for transport) and less responsible. Adam Smith believed that the citizen-consumer should be empowered through superior education. Now, should education conflict with the production of malleable consumers, education will lose. Money wants to keep things that way, and is all too eager to add the selling-point – in the teenage and adult (and post-Viagra, elderly) years – of sex.

III Sex, or Ms. MacDonald's Profession

Why isn't Scottish Enterprise nominating Margaret MacDonald as Scots Businesswoman of the Year? Ok, Wendy's big sister she is not, and Scottish only by parentage, but look at the figures! When les flics moved in on her at the Hotel Tivoli, Paris, they found thirteen mobile phones and a laptop database directing 452 high-grade callgirls and thirty callboys, personally recruited, and charging a standard rate of €1000 a go. 40% of this went back to Cybermadam Mac.

This calls for some statistics. Assuming her 482 staff landed only one client a day, the turnover would still be €3,400,000 a week, or €178,600,000 a year. So the 40% to Mme. MacDonald realises a minimal annual income of €71,000,000 (£42,000,000). Given that her clients, devoted to 'luxury and corruption', will be at it like ferrets, assume several multiples of that. A modest four clients a day, deduct 25% for costs, and you have a net annual income for Mme. Mac of over €210 million.

The sexy bit of our economic life is Michelle Mone and her very own Silicone Glen, the gel-filled bra. But MacDonald seems to have the larger turnover, and is a whizz with new technology: using the mobile, the laptop, and no doubt the numbered, on-line bank account. She has identified (1) her labour force: models and actresses needing the means to shop. (2) her market: wild capitalists with bonuses, big cars, and no absorbing interest in morality. She seems (3) to have avoided the thugs, pimps and drug dealers who make the lives of Scots prostitutes nasty and short. She has not (4) had to donate anything to New Labour.

Nothing original in the above rationalisation. I got it from Bernard Shaw, writing *Mrs Warren's Profession* in 1893. Mrs Warren was offered honest employment making the sulphur matches which killed her sister. Instead she used her good looks to good effect, and invested the proceeds in real estate: a chain of well-run brothels. She is queening it on her Surrey estate when her daughter Vivie, unwisely sent to Cambridge, uses her education to work out where the cash is coming from.

The more you compare him with teenage Trotskyites and Chicago neo-classicists (the two, these days, can be interchangeable) the sharper Shaw seems. Classical economics finds little theoretical space for tourism or Mrs Warren (crime, vice, drugs, etc.). But this pair are *the* major international businesses. The heavy economics journals are equally unforthcoming about the world of 'financial services', or the internationalisation of chartered accountancy which has turned the world's most boring men into a bunch *who speaka like dis.*

Should we be surprised if Gordon Brown's economy goes from golden coach to pumpkin overnight? Shaw wouldn't be. Light on metal-bashing – where classical economics, sure, has its place – the British economy is rich in effervescent enterprises whose precise shape is probably best left to Irish dramatists with a taste for social policy to find out. Anyone for Lloyds, Marconi, Railtrack, Vodafone, Stagecoach? In comparison with this lot Ms MacDonald's business seems positively gold-plated.

What has happened is that, under the hype of neo-classicism, the essential lego-brick of the market economy, the firm, has been smashed to bits. Firms are miniature state-systems: to prosper, they have to limit the role of the market in their own internal organisation, something it's difficult for the boys in red braces to sympathise with, let alone comprehend. So, fortunes have been made in the City by the usual cycle – takeovers, 'realising operational synergies' (making hundreds redundant), 'concentration on core activities' (making thousands redundant), 'management buy-outs' (more cash for the City), and 'attracting inward investment' (flogging what's left to the Germans).

So Ms. MacDonald's concentration on her core activity appears even wiser as Broon's Potemkin economy collapses. She'll do a couple of years, with time off for good behaviour – and retire to savour her millions – she's unlikely to blow it on toyboys. Her enterprise was exactly the sort of thing Ruskin satirised, as well as Shaw. If profit is your only criterion, you know where you'll end up. Though better, perhaps, to have the cash distributed among pretty ladies (it would have been nice to see some going to poor Monica Coghlan, crucified as a perjurer by England's cheekie chappie Jeffrey Archer) than being grabbed by whatever profitable concern pumps hard-core porn into our classier hotels. Perhaps she could give a talk or two at the Strathclyde Business School.

Sex in general seems almost to exist for the churches, and the Catholic church in particular, to work themselves into a state about. Marriage isn't canonic but conventional – and was always pretty irregular in Scotland. Sex is going to happen, like death and taxes; but more fun. Naomi Mitchison, tiny and ancient, flattened demure BBC Scotland interviewerMary Marquis when asked what she regretted in a long life: 'I'm sorry I didn't sleep with more men.' Yet there's a rampant commercialism and debasement: sex as a noisy form of redistribution within our social lottery: the MacDonald-type operators who prised millions out of Becker and Beckham, using tabloids, TV and the courts. The degeneracy of the press and entertainment, the sexualisation of the young: the web has made this a vast, international business, in which growing numbers of the already insecure are being trapped, and in which the winners can buy legal power to get them out of trouble, as their clientele go for bigger and more exciting kicks.

But there's also – visible in the lurid mags and chicklit – a turbo-capitalism of sex, in which the goal isn't what D.H. Lawrence called 'tenderness' but expenditure. This isn't just the bum'n'tit of *GQ*-type mags, whose philosophy is roughly 'jerk off in a big car' – masturbation manuals for white van man – but for girls' mags which quite consciously stress 'junking your man' and making yourself over for the next: an anarcho-version of Betty Friedan's 'feminine mystique'. I and my Berlin colleague Christiane Eisenberg had the wheeze of getting our students to do a content analysis of German and British *Cosmopolitan*. They discovered that German *Cosmo* had 16 pages of editorial on work, and 16 on sex; British *Cosmo* had 30 pages on sex and two on work, advising 'shag the boss'. But all this required constant outgoings on cosmetics, skin care, alcohol, restaurant meals, fashion, lingerie, holidays, phones, pop music. Once your man had been processed into your ex, the process resumed, and the men in suits rubbed their hands. (The stats are, according the *Herald*, 10,000 divorces per annum at £13,000 the go, or £130 million: factor *that* into our housing crisis.)

Mock ye not, *Scotsman* or *Herald* scribe: have a look at the content of your Saturday issue, and the toothsome if not always talented totty on display, thanks to the Hollywood or rag trade PR men, and the supermarket of possibilities erected around it. Cost out the sequences of expenditure, from the first meeting of the eyes to bed. . . to the next meeting of the eyes. Mellors and Lady Chatterley, puritan souls, got it for free.

IV 'Only Individuals and Families'

That, of course, was the point at which She went gyte. 'There is no such thing as society. . .' with 'families' clumsily tacked on. There she was, on top of an ideological skyscraper, batting the biplanes of the Scots kirk. Thatcher was a conventional politician with a crudely-effective tactical sense (put your wet ministers in the spending departments, and watch them tear lumps out of each other), a paralysed opponent, and a ten-year run of luck. As a philosopher she wasn't there at all. Had she been, she might have made something out of the 'families' add-on, which her bright constitutional adviser Ferdy Mount knew something about. I'll show you how.

Asperger's Syndrome, also known in Germany as the *Gelehrtenkrankheit* or 'disease of the wise' was isolated by a Viennese neurologist in the 1940s, his cases being individuals who showed remarkable facility in science and the arts, such as philosophy and architecture, but were almost catastrophically deficient in the social skills. Asperger traced this to a particular physical development within the brain, whereby the zones concerned with cognition and logic were remarkably well-developed, but those concerned with social recognition and empathy were not. Ludwig Wittgenstein was cited as a classic case, a remarkable architect as well as a philosopher, but almost impossible to get on with. Robert MacKean's recent study of

Charles Rennie Mackintosh has also attributed to Aspergers' his obsessive designing of houses and restaurants down to the cutlery, and his helplessness without extremely understanding patrons.

There seems to be a Scots tendency to this: the dirt and divinity scene: Robert Burns (lyrical fluency, philosophic grasp coupled with sexual incontinence), Sir Walter Scott (spontaneous ability to write/neurasthenic conservatism), James Hogg (psychological insight and brilliance as parodist/uncouthness), Hugh Miller (photographic memory, instant literary reactivity/ terrific depressions), Hugh MacDiarmid and Grassic Gibbon (synoptic scope, heteroglossia/political incompetence) and perhaps in our own day R.D. Laing (even though his formal psychiatric doctrine with its stress on nurture rather than nature would deny this) or Alasdair Gray's *Lanark*.

But specifically *Scottish*? Aspergers seems to grow where there's a confluence of folk of similar genetic capabilities – like California's Silicon Valley, given its magnet-like attraction for Intergeek, but with outcomes which slip over from geeky obsession to outright autism. Perhaps the caste-like function of the Scots advocates, clergy and literati in the eighteenth century accelerated this, producing polymathic types like the anthropologist Lords Kames and the linguist Lord Monboddo. Scotland tolerated these eccentrics – or at least a greater proportion of them than elsewhere, while Scots anthropologists from Adam Ferguson onwards prudently studied 'exogamous' marriage as a means of controlling the gene-pool.

The French social anthropologist Emanuel Todd (himself of Scots descent) argues in *The Conditions of Progress* (1989) that a particular family type could turn this sort of thing into social advantage. He argues for a 'Celtic' type of 'authoritarian' family against the English 'affective', nuclear family. By 'authoritarian' Todd doesn't mean dominated by a terrifying patriarch but an association combining blood-relationship and community and taking essentially political decisions. This, with its 'professional' members' – hereditary doctors, lawyers, bards and teachers – could tolerate and socialise the gifted as part of the stock or

47

property of the family/clan. The 'affective' nuclear family pattern, as Lawrence Stone argues in *The Family, Sex and Marriage in England, 1500-1800* (1977), foregrounded romance, sexual love and kindred affection, but could also promote stresses of intimacy which could blow the whole relationship apart.

History would add to the anthropology the ability of the 'Scotlanders' to hammer out forms of agreed coexistence. Mediation between five ethnic groups – Picts, Scots, Angles, Britons, Norse – constituted the country's uniqueness in the early middle ages. It didn't rule out violence, but in practice provided a hard-and-fast way of mitigating it. This found continuing expression in various forms of 'covenant' ideology, from the late medieval 'bond of manrent' to the seventeenth-century 'federal Calvinism' which in due course assimilated religious to civil and commercial law. So the gifted weren't foredoomed to thrawnness. The politician William Ewart Gladstone managed to combine enormous powers of assimilating information – photographic memory, again – with mathematical skill and a powerful sexuality which he sublimated into the cause of liberal economic and constitutional reform. The sociologist and planner Patrick Geddes had similar intellectual virility, which he summed up in his 'triads' – 'heart, hand and head', 'sympathy, synopsis, synergy', 'makers, movers, menders', strengthened by his early training as a banker. Both men were from mixed Highland/Lowland backgrounds and gathered round them a 'family' of retainers which transformed individual qualities into collective effort. Here organisational theory, like Anthony Jay's *Corporation Man* (1972) which he based on his BBC career, with its concentration on internally federative twelve-groups (Lord Reith if not Jesus Christ as management theorist!) could be helpful. It certainly worked in Walter Perry's Open University, 1969-1980, derived from the BBC paradigm.

This suggests that in autonomous Scotland the authoritarian family ought to be rediscovered, while the nuclear family might simply have been a passing phase – 1918-1968: late industrialisation plus the welfare state. It's been kept going by consumerist pressures – advertising, retailing, and their assimilation to populism: that dreadful 'Why we love. . .' of PR-driven mediocrity – but is inflexible, unstable and ultimately irresponsible. Ultimately it can't encourage, or even cope with, the individual qualities that make for innovation, or even the trust and sympathy that a stable society requires. And perhaps, in Scotland, it never has done.

V Migration

In 2001 Scots self-confidence got a shock when an agitation, carefully fanned by the *Daily Record* broke out against asylum seekers. A young Iranian was stabbed to death in a Glasgow scheme, only to be denounced by the paper as an 'economic migrant'. Yet a couple of years later the First Minister actually set out to encourage economic migration, realising that the labour force to sustain the country's prospective pensioner mountain would need to be boosted by 600,000 plus by 2020. In fact, with the exception of desperately poor states threatened anyway by violence, in-migration is usually a spur to economic development. In the nineteenth century the USA grew through its 'huddled masses, yearning to be set free'. Post-war Germany was similarly aided, first by refugees flocking in from Silesia and the DDR, later by *gastarbeiter* coming from Mediterranean countries to take over low-paid work in traditional industries, both reducing the general wage-bill and also enabling existing skilled labour to be retrained. The same can be said of the Nationalist Chinese impact on Taiwan, and most recently the Hong Kongers' impact on British Columbia.

The Scots, as Willie McIlvanney observed, are a mongrel nation. We were rather good at it, and the covenant tradition was essentially a civic method of mediating between them. In the industrial revolution we became more mongrel yet, with Irish, Italian, Lithuanian and Polish incomers, not to speak of English and Welsh coming north, at both ends of the scale. John Roebuck and the Houldsworths were English, Robert Owen Welsh. All of our in-migrant communities have contributed distinctively to Scots life. We are unlikely to be picky when we need immigrants to save our lives, while the cash they remit will in due course enhance the economic reliability of their native countries: a little-researched characteristic which we ought to know far more about.

The rich, anyway, still have no great difficulty in migrating. Every year there are 100,000 visitors from Saudia Arabia with £200 million to spend. Such travellers are not rich in qualifications or intellect, but certainly in money, so no barriers are erected before them: they drive the London retail-go-round; they buy up property, gamble at casinos, drink expensive booze. Their wives buy expensive couture clothes or branded goods, conveying private prestige in a repressive society. Apart from the inevitable Mohammed al-Fayed, few rich orientals drift up north. Of Prince Jefri of Brunei, nothing much creditable can be said, save that he almost single-handedly kept Rolls Royce Motors afloat for several years.

By definition, all of this imported loot is going to stay in the south, as the facilities for enjoying it are many and varied, with no questions asked. We're left with a position in which Prince Jefri is regarded as an unalloyed benefit, as he spends without regard to nationality; Dr Patel is questionable, his utility to us and his prospects of living well have to be set against his disutility to his own people who have been taxed to pay for his education. Mr Elam is hurt, frightened and persecuted, but can do little for us; on a Prince Jefri case he would be turned back; but this would be an abdication of moral responsibility.

Given non-coercive regimes at home, the case against permanent immigration rests on the utility of a highly trained specialist labour force to its own people. We are buying an alleviation of our own problems, for instance in the health service, by depriving poor countries of the professional skills that can sustain them or, perhaps worse, we are creating a professional class whose expectations are so far above national average income to make them a sort of fifth column on our behalf. On the other hand, speaking as an economic migrant myself, it's possible to contribute to both communities, and even derive an additional strength, a synergy, from doing so. We can and should create active partnerships in which we reinforce the skills we need, but also supply expertise for our partners. An engineer in Slovakia needs work, but he also needs English. There's one limb of a barter agreement; another could come from a third party, one of the hi-tech German or French regions, which can adapt conventional engineering to computer control. The payoff for the hi-tech region comes in an opening for its exports.

VI Retirement: or Scotland's Face is her Misfortune

In 2003 I found myself trying to organise a celebration of the 200th anniversary of William Symington's *Charlotte Dundas* steam tug – the world's first practical steamer, and so really the beginning of our modern love-affair with mechanical traction. The result was something of an eye-opener: proof of how far the industrial tide had receded. In 1962, when I was 18, there fell the 150th anniversary of Henry Bell's *Comet*: the first commercially successful steamer, celebrated widely, and with the launch of a replica (now marooned on the edge of a car park in Port Glasgow). Much help was indeed forthcoming, but little from people who were actually in work.

One of the oddities of the economic scene is the failure to transfer useful concepts from neighbouring disciplines. So the ideas of 'voice' and 'exit' popular among political scientists in determining loyalty to institutions, don't turn up in economics, although they're surely important in assessing the strength of things like the firm. One can argue, however, that 'voice' in the branch-plant economy of Scotland is likely to be pretty limited, while 'exit' is almost pre-programmed, given certain conditions. Exit usually involves a shift to an altogether more pleasant Scotland, of villages and small towns, golf courses, yachting, the gentle politics of heritage and nature conservation. Family life – often quite complex in these days of divorce and remarriage – can be for the middle-aged something close to a full-time occupation.

So in place of a life fulfilled in work – the teacher surrounded by his or her pupils; the businessman growing his firm; the professional rising in his organisation – comes the notion of 'going through the motions', accumulating capital, and when convenient either seeking promotion, usually abroad, or cashing in and taking early retirement. In the case of my own generation, this happened around 55, arguably at exactly the point where a mature executive or academic can pass on his expertise to a new generation.

So Scotland's *kleine heile Welt* is deceptive: it is the semi-utopia of people who have been pushed out with golden handshakes before they have managed to strengthen the society which created them. It probably also has the conservative effect that they try to protect their own environment at the cost of a later generation's life-chances. In other words there is a patina of civic identity in small-town Scotland which conceals an absence of real commitment, and will probably result in the longer term in the use of imported resources which come cheaper and cheaper, and the exploration of economic opportunities which are anything but moral.

VI Old Age

'Age, and the only end of age. . . ': there's a gloomy quote from Philip Larkin for every occasion. We don't want to make retirement such a disruptive transition that people are speeded towards the grave. Hence the importance of training for a different sort of life, and in many ways a more rewarding one. My neighbour in Wales died at 94, active to the last. She was retired as long almost as long as she was employed as a teacher, and acted as the centre of her village community: a carer to her mother, who died at over 100, a granny to many children, a gardener, a local historian or more properly remembrancer. An interesting life will make for a productive retirement, so it's worth investing in it.

Yes, we have a continual litany of politicians' talk about pensions and hospitals but little appreciation of older people as a resource, something that is no more of a burden than childhood, and perhaps much less of a burden than yoof. To enable elderly people to live in the centre of active communities, to provide them with accessible shops and libraries and transport, can be a means of stimulating technology and creating jobs. For example, IBM is developing a computer-education programme for pre-schoolers called 'Kidsmart'. In fact, the need for a cognate programme called Gransmart or some such is every bit as pressing, and could probably sustain itself financially. Not only that, for many of us wrinklies the beginnings of incapacity come with new technology that we can't fathom (most of it, given the Martian in which the instructions are usually written). Which is something that suggests an automatic partnership between old(ish) folk and the young, economically and socially profitable to both.

The business of financing this need not be difficult (the over-65s control over 30% of our community wealth) given the prioritising of social housing, to ease the transition from a car-dependent family house to somewhere smaller, though not necessarily quieter – old folk like bustling town centres and prefer to be in communities rather than on their own. True, we have free transport – though they might rather prefer to pay a nominal charge for a service tailored to their needs than thole the present 'take it or leave it' of irregular and unpredictable bus services, seatless and timetable-less shelters. The quality of the care of the helpless is something that depends on the ethic of a society – something that can be alleviated to some extent by a civilian service programme – but this is a problem that can be kept in bounds by not allowing the potentially able to slip towards this state through neglect and inconsiderate planning.

ii. Sectarian Nation

I Religion and Economic Development

Scots sectarianism is one of our most boring and unhelpful traditions – not least because it has accompanied a relentless secularisation since the 1960s when our piety, Protestant and Catholic, seemed remarkable in a secular if not anti-clerical Europe. Piety waned among Protestants from the 1960s and among Catholics from the 1980s, but it's left behind both at populist and intellectual level something like the memory of an amputated limb.

The historiography is ambiguous. Tom Devine says the Catholic Irish saw themselves as Scottish by 1914 though a 'bourgeois' anti-Catholicism persisted until the 1960s, with damaging economic and social effects. A theologically conservative Catholicism – mixing authoritarianism and social radicalism rather like Pope John Paul II himself – distanced Scotland both from the liberal Catholicism of the Continent and the Irish economic boom, then the collapse in vocations and scandals of authoritarianism and sexual misbehaviour left the Church weak and sensitive.

Baden-Württemberg is as divided, in terms of religion, as Scotland. But is there any significant difference between the economic development of mainly Catholic and mainly Protestant areas, their social values, the attitude of their youth? Surely significant, in the culture that educated Max Weber. Swabia was a cradle of the Reformation; Baden and Hohenzollern traditionally Catholic. Swabia was somewhat more innovative in the early phase of industrialisation, suggesting parallels between entrepreneurialism in Central Scotland and Highland/Irish backwardness. But just as on closer exception the Celts were as innovative as the Saxons, there was a wave of immigration (again mixed) after 1945: mainly Catholic from Silesia, and later mainly Protestant from the ex-DDR. An 'emergency industrialisation' came into play, perhaps (as Dr Ya-Fe Hsui has suggested) parallel to the industrialisation of Taiwan after 1945, mainly by nationalist migrants from mainland China. In the Baden-Württemberg case the main motor of this was literally the car industry and German immigrants were rapidly supplemented by *Gastarbeiter* from Turkey, Yugoslavia, Greece and Italy. Maybe the cross (with all its memories and perversions) was replaced by the Mercedes-Benz star!

Scotland's problem may have been that this phase of 'neo-industrialisation' 1945-1973 was weaker and could not cope with the collapse of jobs in the heavy industries. The Baden-Württemberg transition was mainly from small-farmer agriculture to farmer-workers who let out their land to a commercial tenant, expanded the farmhouse into a multi-occupation dwelling, and commuted by bus and car to the new factories. As a result housing stock was far superior, and the political ethos conservative and cooperative. In Scotland the ghosts of old economic élitism sought new homes.

II Kick football into touch?

'Where are you from?'
'Stuttgart.'
'Zat near Berlin?'
'No.'
'Germany. . . Berti fuckin' VOGTS!.'

The man-on-the-train with the clinking plastic bag – thirty going on seventy – in the twenty minutes before he lapsed into unconsciousness. He had me doing my Erich von Stroheim accent, anything to avoid bringing up his obsession. He was as they say 'good natured', so incoherent I couldn't make out which of the Old Firm teams he supported, and he gave up trying to enlighten me. But what an idiot!

£400 million a year is spent by the Scots on football, almost wholly on watching it, and paying the Prince of Darkness himself, Rupert Murdoch, who has been raking it in from his satellite channels. Less good news for the business of Scottish football, which with the exception of the colossi of the West seems in perhaps terminal financial trouble, for the Scottish economy and indeed for Scottish sport. A PR-propelled masque of the undead has imported gladiators from societies utterly remote from Glasgow's ancient feuds – and they pick up millions from the business. Some of them are said to remit the cash to their relatives in the third world, sustaining whole communities – and the best of luck to them! – others blow it on booze, drugs and girls. The goings-on at the Roman Colosseum were infinitely nastier, but we're getting there.

It will be apparent that I don't give a toss about football loyalties. I went to a match once, in 1956, Hearts versus Motherwell, a one-all draw. I liked it, but had no wish to see another. There are hundreds of thousands like me, who would sympathise with Cliff Hanley when he put in his *Who's Who* entry: 'Every human activity, except sport'. We see the guff about 'the beautiful game' as a means of getting people to shell out big bucks to gawp, while being robbed of the pitches and the health to play the game for themselves, by smart – and often none-too-scrupulous business gents and no-brain journalists.

What sort of football do we want to have? A lot of small, local teams to play in leagues which reflect the desire to train, and to demonstrate the health of the community. And the mastodons? If merchandising pulls in most footie income, isn't it obvious that most Old Firm merchandise is toxic? If the game is to be compared to fine wine (yawn) then this stuff is Buckie on draught. Football developed to counterbalance a grim industrial reality. But if we're going to have a society oriented round the play ethic, then the emphasis must be on participation: which involves building up sports organisations and facilities, not closing them down at the rate that has recently been going on. And if we're going to go on from the Tartan Army to carnival, then let's have a proper Carnival, a fest running from Advent through to Lent – from St Andrews Day through a detoxed Christmas (away with family feuding/pigging it in front of the box!), an all-weather Hogmanay, to Burns Night – with something for everyone, generating goodwill, visitors and lots of jobs

III To be a Pilgrim

Sectarianism coexists with perhaps Europe's most materialist society, where the intellect associated with theology, the communal life of the Churches, the music and power of the liturgy, have all been dissipated. Mammon, not God, persuaded Sir Peter Burt in 1999 to sign up the Rev Pat Robertson for the Bank of Scotland, a sharp rightwing financier who believed that the End of the World would come in 2007. Luckily Robertson decided that we were a dark land in which homosexuality was tolerated, and flounced off before he could have a heart-to-heart with Cardinal Winning.

Religion may have been debatable, but always had cultural compensations; its successors have varied from the weird to the despicable, but on the whole they have preserved the nastiness, not the culture or its consolations.

We come back to the business of reconstructing an order that will sustain us, something for which the economic arguments are generally positive. If it doesn't move mountains, the sociologists tell us that faith stabilises and makes rational.

'Herr, red' auf mich, dass mein Leben ein Sinn hat'. 'Lord, convince me that my life means something': the great plea of the soloist in Brahms' *German Requiem* is still as rational as its music is glorious. Consolation: the mysticism in religion is still valuable, our presence on this planet being baffling enough; and the legacy in Christanity in music, literature and art is still magnificent, as even fierce critics like MacDiarmid and Larkin would attest. Secular replacements, from Positivism to our current crop of prophylactics, from dieting to astrology, have generally bombed.

We are, paradoxically, more likely to gain the respect of other religions by being strong enough in our own to speak a common language. Community: the absolute element in religion has rightly been exposed and criticised, but the capacity of Christians to care, and to draw on the resources of tradition to do so, remains relevant, particularly in an ageing society. The almshouse, the monastic community and the hospice are resting places more durable than we thought. Economically, the pilgrimage is probably something that we in Scotland can make something of: as with the popularity of the pilgrim trails from France to Santiago de Compostella. Even for the unbeliever, this journey to the heart of the mystery, coupled with the appreciation and intoxication of the tradition – be it the *Book of Kells* or the Bruckner *Te Deum*, the austere cells of the Celtic monks or the treasury of hymns and psalms which remains intriguingly common to both religious traditions – this tradition can recharge resources. If commercialised faith in the USA is probably the nearest we can get to devil-worship, we have to save Christianity from the Christians.

iii Deconstructing Broon

I Upwardly mobile phones

In mid-2002 trade minister Patricia Hewitt was interviewed in *Der Spiegel* about all the things Germany was doing wrong. To go from Germany with its new trains and buses, environmental policies and bright students to Britain has always been a somewhat hallucinatory experience; but New Labour's insistence that its ramshackle realm was some sort of economic miracle made the feeling more extreme. Hewitt's claim was grounded on growth (2.2% to Germany's 0.6% in 2001) and unemployment (5.1% to Germany's 8.1%).

But what about mobile phones? In Tübingen, if you use one, you get slung off the bus. In Britain, you can't escape their trills, and the amateur soap opera that a people once famous for reserve treat you to. Germans certainly buy them (61% against 71% Britons had one in early 2002) but, as with their cars, don't use them as much. What effect did they have on economic growth?

I looked up 'mobile phones' in government surveys of household expenditure and got nowhere, but it's always some time before a new enterprise or consumer good gets into the official statistics. The Central Office of Information's *Britain 2001* had one entry on 'mobile phones' saying that in 1998-9 25% of households had one (giving a number of 6 million); and later on another, for 2000, detailing the customers of the main networks, which gave a number of 30.7 million. The time-limits were fuzzy, but this suggested that between early 1999 and the summer of 2000, 24.7 million people bought mobile phones, paid connection charges, and ran up bills. What did this cost? I still recollect the indrawn breath when my daughter's One-to-One account turned up, but let's assume £500 a year.

So: £500 multiplied by 24.7 million gives £12.35 billion. Set against total Gross Domestic Product for 2000 of £891 billion, this comes to 1.4%, in a year which saw 2.9% growth. Knock off the 0.4% (balancing a phone-growth period of about 16-18 months, rather than a year, against phone bills estimated for a year) and you still have a third of Britain's growth coming from mobile phones. Are they an asset, or something between a toy and a narcotic, a disruptive invasion of the reflective time needed to calculate economically? We don't yet know.

But did it help our Gordon! Brown's genius – and here the boy really done good – wasn't to sit hand in hand with Prudence on the sofa, but to have uninhibited sex with the City. Borrowing an Institute of Economic Affairs whizz – suggested but never much used in North Sea Oil – he auctioned off 'third-generation' phone licences at the top of the dot-com boom in March-April 2000, banking over £20 billion in exchange for empty space, or at least for facilities actually worth perhaps £3 billion. Bernie Ecclestone, look to your laurels! Then he let British 'new technology' (the hardware was almost exclusively imported) launch itself on Rhenish capitalism in the takeover by Vodafone of Mannesmann in 2001. Christopher Gent, John Major's smarter brother, sweet-talked the Mannesman board into a betrayal of their 'social partners' whose demoralisation can't be underestimated.

II Not counting sickies. . .

Otherwise, nothing was quite what it seemed. British unemployment was 3 points under that of Germany in December 2001. In a paper delivered to the British Association and reported in the *Guardian* on 5 September, David Webster, of the LSE and now Glasgow's Director of Housing, estimated that 'long-term sickness' could account for 7.0% out of work, compared with 2.1% in Germany and 0.3% in France. People were moving from claiming unemployment benefit to claiming sickness benefit as the terms of the former were made more rigorous; something borne out by recent complaints by GPs at being overburdened by issuing sick notes. If we allow for such socio-medical factors as drug addiction, something like three times the German level, teenage pregnancies and their consequences, and the connection between poverty (about 20% compared with 10% in Germany) and ill-health, the case for a level of unemployment above that of Germany – Webster's figures would suggest 12% against 10.2% – seems strong.

Still, the Scottish workforce is a bigger proportion of population than that of Baden-Württemberg (45.6% of population against 36.3%) Hold on, is that 'full-time workers'? Er, no. Of Scotland's 2.3 million workers nearly 600,000 (25.8%) are part-time. The Baden-Württemberg number is 585,000 out of 3.9 million or 15% (though the Germans have only just admitted that 85% of cleaning ladies are unregistered). Unsurprising then that the decrease in actual poverty has been, to put it mildly, gentle.

As for training: 25% of Scottish teenagers leave school at 16 without qualifications; in Germany this is 9.1%. Most school leavers go into some form of apprenticeship as *Auszubildende* or *Azubis*, while the Scottish record in such areas as 'modern apprenticeships' has been patchy. And *these* amount to only 5% of the age cohort. Jamieson and Peat were worried about this in 1999, largely attributing it to the lack of medium-sized enterprises (only 13% of employees were in firms of between 50-249 employees, compared with about 25% in Ba-Wü). They ought to be even more worried now.

III The world through blunted sight

'What people don't realise,' a Brown trusty said over drinks, 'is how blind Gordon is.' Brown's clouded sight isn't unique among Chancellors. Gladstone's brilliant neo-classical ally, Bob Lowe, was afflicted as an albino. Patrick Trevor-Roper, the opthalmologist, commented on some of the – often positive – cultural consequences of this in his *The World through Blunted Sight* (1988). David Blunkett is quite obviously blind, but blind people develop their own methods of replicating sight. The partially-sighted are in a different situation: certain types of visual information come over and are interpreted – television, trusted associates. Others scarcely come over at all: appraisals of environments or city streets, of collective emotion: the sense you get after walking through some new smiley-happy town mall that (a) there are no local names on the shops and (b) there are an awful lot of for sale notices in the adjoining streets. . .

Patrick Geddes used to 'read' a town by walking through it, or taking a tram right out into the far suburbs and the countryside. Much of this book has stemmed from similar activity, as a means of questioning statistical series and received opinion. This is something one quickly encounters in Lloyd George's economic politics, but not in the academically brilliant Brown. The resulting logical dogmatism may be connected to the Asperger's phenomenon (see II.i) and its homogenising in Scotland by the extended family. 'Family', in this sense, has always been important to Brown, but it radically altered its meaning with the move south.

The figures around the Chancellor – Ed Balls, Douglas Alexander – are far different from those in his Scottish years. The Bank of England had effectively been nationalised in 1917 by another dour Scot, Andrew Bonar Law, to finance wartime industry in Clydeside and elsewhere. Far from being a decentralist step, Brown's liberation of it in 1997 passed its control to the hands of the City, not best known for its interest in industry. 'It is through manufacturing that we will succeed or fail' wrote young Broon in *Where there is Greed* (1989). And now?

The move south was also accompanied by an ideological change, towards American paradigms. Brown's European interests were anyway slight, but he now took to spending his summers on the North-East coast and absorbing the 'intervention-lite' and welfare into work' ethos of the Clinton era. A means of distinguishing himself from Blair's apparent friendliness to Europe, and checking the Premier's alliance with Rupert Murdoch? The resulting grudge fight in which the two principals have varying advantages to deploy over one another, and calm is sustained by bilateral negotiations, has seen a galloping de-technologising of British society. The call-centre won out over the expensive reconstruction of the railway system. With results that we now see. The pillars of New Labour society seem as shoogly as its principles.

But back to low German growth. I can remember the 1970s, the Club of Rome, and the popularity in left-green circles of redistribution and conservation over 'crude rises in GDP'. Germany recycles four times more waste than Britain, solar and combined-cycle power cuts fuel consumption, photo-voltaic cells are being mass-produced and so plummeting in price, bus and public-transport ridership is up dramatically (in Tübingen by over 40% in the last four years: in Britain it's fallen 30% since 1970). But in national accounting, these are going to show up as *minuses* in the growth rate. Germany has its problems, chiefly the East: no longer surreptitiously injecting manufacture into the old Bundesrepublik, but a lot of stroppy fellow-citizens, and a two-million increase in population as a result of *Spätaussiedlers* arriving from the old Soviet Union and not integrating much. Hi-tech industry means an obsessive tendency to build ingenious machines (to issue all your rail tickets and do all your banking) which eliminate jobs. But, after a bit of prowling around the statistics, I am coming to see these as manageable compared with the prospects before Broon's Britain.

'Today UK roads and railways are congested, our airports and airways uncomfortably and sometimes dangerously crowded, road and rail maintenance in disarray and safety now a major issue in the public mind.'

That was Broon, but in 1989, alas. Despite a commitment to sustainable development, Scots road traffic alone rose between 1993 and 2002 by 18%.

iv Death by Carbon: Oil and Transport

I Black stuff, bleak future

In the last hour of the millenium, Hurricane Lothar hit west Europe. Whole mountainsides in the Black Forest were shaved of their trees. Nothing to do with us? The millions of tons of windfall timber blew a hole in the economics of Scots forestry which has taken longer to clean up than the debris. In the summer of 2003 the 'hitze' saw temperatures from Edinburgh to Seville soar to around 100^0 fahrenheit. Was this the inevitable consequence of global warming and the doom of what Patrick Geddes had called the Paleotechnic age, when we had let the demon of carbon power out of the box without being able to control it?

Neo-liberals disputed this, and they had laid on their own spectacular, when the 'hop on a plane like a bus' habit of America allowed a couple of score Moslem fanatics to turn commuter jets into deadly guided missiles, on 9/11. An unusually primitive US government – only just elected by dubious means – proclaimed a crusade against terror (selectively defined). Others saw this as a desperate means of securing the oil reserves it required, not just from Iraq but from the Caspian Sea, where a rise in militant Islam could bring the whole 'heartland' region under threat.

Scotland had been here before, and not just because of the North Sea oil boom after 1970. The real breakthrough of Clyde shipbuilding and engineering in the Victorian era was the creation of the delivery mechanisms for the coal – machinery, railways, ships – on which industrialisation depended until World War II. The problem was the 'Upas Tree' effect: a huge industry – if unplanned – absorbs or prices out the resources which might produce a more balanced economy. Likewise, oil wasn't the economic rescuer that it could have been, and in social-democratic Norway was; but Scotland's historical experience and endowment at least meant that there was some sort of social dividend from it, and that it didn't corrupt the state. Nigeria, with vast reserves, has by contrast simply been pillaged by the companies in cahoots with a venal élite, and the same is likely to occur in the ex-USSR.

After *Fool's Gold* and its TV series I don't want to repeat myself, but some updating points must be made. First, the fluctuations in oil price have gone. In 1996 the US Delphi Institute was forecasting the $20 barrel for 2016, but when Scotland voted in 1999 North Sea production (at its all-time peak of 3 million barrels per day) was yielding under $10 dollars a barrel, or about $11 billion per annum. This did no favours to the SNP. But the price is now $33 a barrel, dragging in $23 billion. Middle Eastern instability and Chinese industrialisation are still pushing the price up, so even with a decline in North Sea output to 1.3mbd in 2010 (though qualified by new technology which prolongs the life of fields) there is still, for Scotland, a lot of money to be played for – given a $40 barrel about $19 billion.

II Close the lot down?

One of the advantages of a service-industry economy ought to be a reduction in pollution levels, but this has been more than outweighed by increases in car and plane use. Even when engineering is producing the 3-litre-per-100-km car, the growth of motoring (9% in 1992-2002: BaWü, which makes the things, stood pat) has been skewed towards huge people-carriers and SUVs, in which mummy can play at being Arnold Schwarzenegger, when taking Sophie and Toby to school. As for the physical condition of the home-and-car-bound tots, the bill for mass-obesity will come in, and it will be high.

What we have had since the 1950s is American-style mobility growth, encouraged by the fact that our technology stretches only as far as car retail and maintenance, which is also the last redoubt of Scottish SME capital – the Chairman of Glasgow Chamber of Commerce, notable advocates of the M74 extension is (surprise, surprise) Duncan Tannahill, a car dealer. So much for sustainable land transport! Air travel however surpassed it and doubled to 19.8 million passengers at Scots airports between 1992-2002. Tax-free fuel, would-be airport cities, and white van man-style publicity has given us the cheapo flights of Ryanair. Do they cost more than the old charter flights they're running out of business? They pollute every bit as much, and Michael O'Leary's politics 'a right-wing Irish dictator' – are less than ecological. But will that prevent our politicians from wanting more of them?

Road-haulage has taken advantage of just-in-time delivery and the fall of the Iron Curtain to undercut other modes with cheap labour and overloaded trucks. *Less* through traffic passed to Europe in 2002 by rail than in 1992, before the Chunnel opened, although the road systems are now breaking down under overload. In Ba-Wü the adaptation of the regionally-planned economy has foregrounded public passenger transport, from the arterial Frankfurt-Stuttgart and Frankfurt-Basel high-speed lines to elaborate local systems in the *Verkehrsverbande* which now cover most of the Land. In 1999 I hosted Sarah Boyack at Freudenstadt when she was the first Scots minister to visit Europe. Late in 2004 the railway from Rastatt to Freuden-stadt, comparable to the Waverley line, was electrified, a project *not even tabled* until 2001.

Germany has the 'advantage' that most of the rail system was in ruins in 1945, had to be rebuilt, and adapted to a two-state system. This included wholesale electrification. Scots railways mainly date from 1840-70 and show their age, with crumbling cuttings, bridges and embankments. The Forth Bridge alone will cost £250 millions to restore, over the next ten years. West Coast Main Line modernisation, as James Meek showed in a merciless *Guardian* analysis, was based on a signalling system so futuristic it didn't exist, and is now at least ten times over its £1.5 billion budget.

So, give up and close the lot down, or like our Canadian or New Zealand cousins, leave a basic freight network with a few trains for the tourists? There's a well-heeled lobby agitating along these lines, including the father of privatisation, Sir Christopher Foster, as well as the Adam Smith Institute. In fact the real cost-overruns haven't been on provincial lines – subsidies in Scotland have actually fallen at current prices from £350 million in 1996 to £250 million today – but on fiascos like the West Coast upgrade.

As it is, devolution would make closures very difficult; and, because Scotland and Wales have pro-rail regimes, they've probably helped the English provincial lines to survive. Labour and the SNP, however, continue to back road schemes, less out of conviction than because motorists *vote* and non-motorists (being poor and alienated) don't. But what if the parties were driven – say by Westminster cuts – to make a choice?

Rail closures, however, would not only conflict with European rail policy, but expose Scotland as a loser in attempts to replan the urban central belt – it's time we faced up to the fact that we waste much of the £9 billion a year we spend on motoring, and that in an efficient industrial economy 30% of business trips ought to be by an efficient and relaxing public transport system. If the laptop is a mobile office, the railway can cater for it (power connections, satellite links) quickly and economically. And if the Swiss can make their rural railways the basis of their high-value-added tourist industry, why not us? Yet we have the paradox of a largely Scots-run Transport ministry, supplemented by further Scots, David Begg and Tom Winsor, at the Commission for Integrated Transport and the Rail Regulator, making a complete horlicks of any possible synergy. The fact that we're too de-industrialised to modernise transport on our own ought to be a challenge to intra-European cooperation, not an excuse for giving up.

v Scotland the Bent

I It's the luxury and corruption show!

Some months ago Ray Gosling went bankrupt, the great historian of that underrecorded Britain of caravan parks, white-van-men, off-licences, bookies' runners, spivs. Apparently the BBC no longer wanted his quirky, affectionate, documentaries. Or maybe Gosling's marginals had now simply become too worrying?

Fast forward to a *Scotsman* survey of Scotland's highest earners in 2002. List-making is the higher trivia, but this one was weird enough. Scotland's top fifty clocked up £115 million. Of these eighteen were footballers, thirteen businessmen, eight in the arts or entertainment, three lottery winners and two lawyers. 'Annual earnings' means of course that the subterranean holdings of Scotland's truly rich don't show up, but what was notable about the fifty – extreme in the case of the lottery winners – was *their* marginality. J.K. Rowling (worth £34 million) was still to peak, but footballers would vanish when that bubble burst. Media folk are the temporary kings of metropolitan caprice. But the winners are the sunny side of a society erected not on industry but on a mixture of speculation and illusion which has smothered civic values.

These two old eighteenth-century *roués*, luxury and corruption, were back, and were having a ball. Jack McConnell is waging war on 'ned culture', attacking the dim, drunken teenagers who annoy Labour's residual loyalists by hanging about, low-level thieving and vandalising. In fact this is in statistical terms a diminishing problem, (in Europe brighter and more together teenagers cause more lasting damage with big, meticulous, and boringly-derivative graffitti) compared with the pitiful lack of opportunity the poor little sods have.

II Our fourth sector

Ian Rankin got into the top hundred earners with about £500,000. Worth it, because he's our Simenon, and in an unnerving way also our Scott, chronicling not the shift from status to contract but in our present dystopia the shift from contract to something more atavistic, almost wholly neglected by our historians and sociologists. If fiction defines the acceptable in behaviour by dissecting the extreme, as that solid citizen Leslie Stephen long ago insisted, then Rankin and Rebus are on this frontier. In *Let it Bleed* Rebus pursued evil-doing right up to the Scottish Office's Permanent Secretary, I thought at the time rather overdoing it. I'm now less certain. There does seem to be a point where the scale and variety of crime – or the toleration of it and its rewards – bids fair to distort the entire society. In Scotland, are we on the way to that?

The details of the huge and horrid monster are familiar enough to tabloid readers as well as Rebus fans. But given the limitations of Scottish journalism, there's no attempt to map its economic dimensions. *Scotland on Sunday* did a longish piece in 2002 on a wealthy Glasgow businessman beaten to death after an apparent falling-out in the minicab business. Since then, silence. Enquiries appear to have got nowhere. A story broke in mid-2003 of a charity fund-raising firm 'Solutions Limited' which pocketed over £10 million raised for Breast Cancer Research in Scotland. This seems to be in suspended animation, or at least sidelined by the Moonbeams kids cancer scam (under £100,000 getting through out of £3 million raised).

Daily Record investigations into various criminal families in the scrap metal, drugs and loan-shark business suggested annual turnovers over £30 millions. A drug smuggler sent down for 21 years got himself transferred after six to an open prison, from which he immediately absconded. After he was found dead in London it appeared he had been a police informer.

Crime is very big business indeed if you extrapolate the linkages which inevitably emanate from our huge drugs problem. In 1981, when I published the first edition of *No Gods and Precious Few Heroes* this scene was small, under 1000 addicts. 2003 estimates suggest around 60,000: per capita, three times greater than Germany. The Scottish Select Committee computed a total impact of £633 million for drugs in Glasgow in 1996: theft, repairs, insurance, policing, imprisonment, unemployment, medication and so on. Adding about 20% for inflation over the last seven years and, grossing-up a Scottish figure, there's perhaps a £2-3 billion impact, or around 5% of Scottish GDP. This is worth more than our agriculture: not just a useful comparison but terrifying in its implications. As manufacturing industry declines, particularly the locally-owned element, any big spender, however dubious, will increasingly call the shots, buy legal and accounting skills, and make itself impregnable.

Drugs help fill in important gaps in our statistics, notably that between registered unemployed and total workless. The percentage of the first in Glasgow is 12% – not brilliant by European standards – but those on 'incapability benefit' bring the workless total up to 30%. Drugs are peculiarly salient, given the headlong rate of deindustrialisation dramatised by places like Craigneuk (which formerly housed the workforce of Ravenscraig steelworks) and the 1940s-built mining village of Drongan. They are supplemented by 'rest-and-recreation' for the stressed-in-work (Fraserburgh and heroin) and the student-clubbing-ecstasy scene.

This traffic accelerates other illegal enterprises, but several of these are doing pretty well on their own. A single issue of the *Herald* (22 December 2003) ran two pieces: one about trading in counterfeit videos and CDs as a speciality of the Glasgow Barras, on which the police didn't seem to be able to lay a finger (a later story on 13 February guesstimated this illegal trade at a billion) and another on a pig-rearer who flouted all the rules, mis-treated his animals, and had still cornered 20% of the Scots market. Add to this the transnational penumbra of smuggling, from fags 'n booze (Customs admit to 3 million fags a day entering through Dover alone) to illegal workers and sex slaves, and the apparent impunity with which much of this is carried on, and much of what Jeremy Rifkin called the 'fourth sector' in his *Age of Access* (1999) seems rather more securely rooted in Scotland than his benign play-ethic-driven 'third sector' which Pat Kane is trying to extend.

Play there is, but not of the altruistic and voluntaristic sort. Add to the above the high-risk areas of pubs, clubs, and dance venues, minicabs and some filling stations, escort agencies and saunas, tanning studios, bookies and casinos – some above board, others not. A *Herald* story about C**** Cabs, the second-largest firm in Scotland, implied that it was dominated by the gangs, employing the officials who were supposed to regulate it – their council department simply vanished in 1995. Garnish with similarly unpredictable security firms, some of which are straightforward protection rackets; (if the total British bouncer population is put at 100,000, this suggests about 8,000 Scots musclemen), moneylenders, scrapyards and waste disposers, and cast an apprehensive eye at the informal economy of Belfast, with its the mutation of sectarian hard men into career criminals of the Johnny Adair sort, not too far away. Scotland's awful recycling statistics are linked to 'waste-disposal' firms which see their clients right by tipping old fridges into the Clyde and tyres (about 4.5 million are discarded annually) into derelict quarries.

III Drink 'n drugs 'n financial services

Can politics and the rule of law be quarantined from such a big economic presence? Huge transactions on the other side of legality – not to mention fraud on government agencies – inevitably affect police, bureaucrats and politicians. For the cops, Rankin's *Resurrection Men* seems, given the recent BBC documentary on the racism and thuggery of the Lancashire police college, mild. Scots lawyers have been notably entrepreneurial, in many ways a plus, but this sets up a tension between profit and professionalism. Inability to shell out fat fees has rarely marked our bigger rascals.

And the politicians? Jack McConnell's had some problems with his constituency party's finances, in which the black economy was almost acrobatic, with the drug-dealing son of a Motherwell Labour benefactor being gunned down not long after being involved in a 'Red Rose' fund-raising dinner which raised an (undeclared) £8000 for the party, promptly embezzled by the treasurer. The *Herald* ran a recent story on a family of villains given permission by North Lanarkshire Council to build a fireworks depot at Newmains which would contain twice the amount of explosive which blew the centre of the Dutch town of Eschede to bits. How did this happen?

Scotland – and Scots lawyers – supposedly pioneered the globalised company. We are now seeing such outfits behaving badly. The authorised version was supposed to show boardroom probity and social conscience of the Coca-Cola sort being exported to the developing or ex-communist world. Remember 1990, when democracy was calculated by the spread of McDonalds? Less instructive examples like the United Fruit Company (of 'banana republic' fame) were rarely quoted.

After Enron, Andersen, etc. (not to speak of Coke's 'Dasani' – Sidcup tapwater with added carcinogens) it's more the case of the City and the CEOs going the way of the uncouth lot in their Buenos Aires or Ibadan branches. Europe-wide haulage concerns like Germany's Willi Betz have been fingered for illegally employing, underpaying and overworking drivers from the old USSR. BAe, which owns most of what's left of Clyde shipbuilding, has for years been up to its eyeballs in bribery in the Middle East and the MoD. Who is behind the fag-smuggling racket but Ken Clarke's BAT, with its huge export trade to midget Andorra? The booze-culture that is threatening much of our youth, helped on by alcopops and happy hours, and policed by the security firms, is sanctioned at brewery boardroom level.

Tom Devine and Michael Fry have recently reminded us

that our robust entrepreneurial past was bound up with smuggling fags (the Tobacco Lords, even if the tobacco was for snuff) and booze (the Whisky Barons) and providing the Chinese with dope (the Hong Kong Taipans). Many a banker or lawyer, looking forward to golden handshake, grandchildren and the fairway, wouldn't, even today, be quite so well-set without winding links which bind him to sink schemes and trainee neds. Indeed the respectable side of Scottish culture, the posh restaurants, jewellery and clothes shops, must owe a lot to 'fourth sector' trade (Johnny Adair and wife's shopping expeditions to Glasgow were legendary), not to speak of lawyers confronted with fat fees, upfront and in cash.

Could it get worse? Yes. There have been reports of the Russian and other East European mafias – who make Cosa Nostra look like kirk elders – buying their way in, leaving the Scots hoods looking squeaky-clean, and with lots of loot to push around. At a lower level, it's fifty years since the American sociologist Rollo May noted that the drug pusher followed classic entrepreneurial logic in methodically growing his business while keeping off the stuff. Now a hip-hop pop culture, unchallenged among the teenies for several years, openly admits and revels in its criminality. Faced with this, our 'rest and recreation culture' – due to be enlarged by Glasgow as Las Vegas with rain – is a sitting duck.

And can we get out? Talking this over with a senior Holyrood figure, we found ourselves reaching the same conclusion. It is our drug problem, proportionate to population one of the biggest in Europe, which is the locomotive of this disorder and only by being uncoupled from it, can its detailed sections be treated and controlled. Prohibition, advertising and Tsars won't work: only legalisation and nationalisation of the drugs trade will. This will be a long and uncomfortable process; it will require a powerful executive and well-supervised administrative and rehabilitation machine; but it will turn off the fuel tap of our criminal culture.

vi. Bank Robbery

I

'Festival fans – come and live in Scotland!' Thank you, Jack. But just possibly the same fans are keen on opera, and have heard the shrieks from your own troupe. It gets worse: this cultural vandalism is being perpetrated by a nation which blows over £400 million (or a hundred times Scottish Opera's losses) on football, watching bright Latvians play a game it can't manage any more. It is being observed by men in suits who trouser in bank or insurance bonuses sums equivalent to Scottish Opera's losses every few months.

The annals of Scottish crime are vast and varied: the hoods – stealing to order for the Russian mafia? – who relieved the Duke of Buccleuch of his Leonardo; Stephen Jupe's Glen Turret Single Malt which brought him £4 million before anyone noticed that there was no distillery in the glen; Lady Rosemary Aberdour (who was neither a Lady nor from Aberdour but who took £3 million from a children's charity to pay for her shopping). There are some mildly diverting blowbacks: the Scotland Yard account-ant who fiddled the plods out of a million to set himself up as the Laird of Tomintoul; Cap'n Bob Maxwell, psychopath *extraordinaire*, who took over North Sea helicopters, the Edinburgh Commonwealth Games, but bankrolled Aberdeen University Press (a Good Thing) before walking the plank.

The Aberdour case is particularly interesting as it would

have been impossible in Sherlock Holmes' time. Then, some roaring old snob would have turned her lorgnette on *Burke's Peerage*, failed to find Lady A, and the game would be up. Nowadays straightforward class-prejudice (which had its rules) is confused by celebrity culture – the survival of Lord Archer being a case in point: sheer chutzpah and the aura of wealth can get you a very long way from fumbling prosecutors, particularly if they've got a bad conscience.

II

This sort of thing happens in Ibsen or Shaw plays where the villain, up against a wall, turns on his *gutbürgerlich* pursuers and exposes all the – genteeler but nastier – things they've been up to, which always makes sorting matters out very troublesome. This came to mind when I did a bit of personal arithmetic on a trusted friend, whose results astonished even me. Since 1962 I have banked out of unthinking patriotism with the Bank of Scotland (first with the British Linen, then the BoS, and now the Halifax BoS). So why not compare the two, in terms of service and charges?

The results were as follows, in a situation where about three-quarters of my cash-flow passes through the Deutsche Bank:

Quarter 1, 2003 (all amounts in sterling)

	Total handled	Charges	as % of total
Deutsche Bank	£21,190	£16.40	0.07
Bank of Scotland	£7,000	£31.35	0.45

The charges of the Bank of Scotland are six times greater than those of the Deutsche Bank, for an inferior service – no customer terminals, no giros, small and expensive overdrafts, and painful mistakes. It took HBOS International over two months, and several reminders, to issue an interest certificate for a Money Market account. To a customer in balance (for once!) the Bank has expressed neither apology nor the slightest degree of concern.

Does HBOS make sense as a long-term lender? When I retire in five years, I want to continue as a consultant in regional studies and distance-learning cooperation. So I sussed out the cost of a loan for the capital equipment I'd need: computers, etc. Say £7,000. West Indian gent from the BoS was only too willing to write me a cheque, annual payment rate of 8.9%. The rate from the Deutsche Bank was 11.24% for an arrangement which would clear my overdraft every month up to a maximum credit of €10,000. But the latter's rate was simple interest (Festzinsen), while the former's was compound. So after six years I would have repaid the loan plus 42% in Germany, and plus 98% in Scotland. The sums in the Harvie saga are tiny, but grossed up for any firm they could be critical.

Deutsche Bank is part of the problem. Its London HQ has a foyer you can lose a Zeppelin in, and not a customer terminal in sight. It's not there to cause grief to the High Street Banks by competing, but to play the casino with the big boys – with whom it wants a rich man's cartel. The citizen customer or manager can get lost.

III

I was moved to hit the calculator not just by private irritation but by an arrogant performance by Sir George Mathewson saying the Royal Bank didn't need the Footsie and Scotland didn't need manufacturing. This came shortly after Susan Rice, of Lloyds TSB – and supposedly a 'Friend of Scotland' – said that outsourcing was super for Scottish financial services. Both, famous for their bonuses, seemed to have their social reflexes running at pretty low power. But more seriously, they were coming from an academic-political-finance Bermuda Triangle in which 'maximising social capital' – or what our small business and trade union sides put as a priority – simply disappears.

The banks made their dough in the 1980s and 1990s from privatisation and the takeover of council housing by mortgage-lenders. All three have run into problems over money-laundering or executive misbehaviour. And in these circumstances, the implication seemed to be that Adam Smith's 'sympathy' went out the window, as these two old *roués* Luxury and Corruption strode in at the door. In 2004, we are seeing the result.

This is surely a case for real investigative action by Parliament: is competition functioning at all in banking, and if not what is this costing us?

My hunch is that, as with retail and accountancy, big doesn't mean efficient but cartelised and politically over-mighty – all the more serious in a lender's market where the borrower is always at a strategic disadvantage.

So what do we do about it? One approach is to generate more competition, particularly from Europe with its lower interest rates. Another is to generate locally, mutually-controlled banking. In 1983 we lost our alternative banking system when Lloyds took over the TSB. The mutuals have since been on the skids, though both in banking and in retail the Co-op, long written off, has made a spectacular recovery. Once housing implodes ordinary folk will want another from of saving, so why not by providing funds at a local level?

And finally there's fire insurance: philanthropy, what the rich did to avoid Hell. The chantries, the patronage of the banker Medicis or Rothschilds, the Usher and MacEwan Halls. The Royal Bank could bankroll Scottish Opera for years and not notice it ; and it could build an Edinburgh-Glasgow bullet train line for a fraction of the cash it has looted from British Rail. Put it this way, Peter Burt and Fred Goodwin: between you and the celestial Muirfield Fairway is a pit full of flames and terrible people. And only generosity will build you a rainbow bridge over it. Carnegie would have thought thus, and possibly because of him American corporations give 10% of their profits to good causes. In Britain, it's 1 %.

III. Culture Nation
i Small state, growing Europe

A new regionalism is rapidly gaining ground at the beginning of the twentieth century, and it is tribal in character. People look for homogeneous units, and thereby turn their backs on the larger heterogeneous nation-states of the nineteenth century. Sometimes they claim that their Catalonia, Slovakia or Wallonia will connect more easily with the globalised network of a new age; but the probability must be high that these allegedly homogeneous regions will in fact resemble Chechnya or Bosnia or other war-torn areas. Intolerance within and aggressiveness without are a frequent concomitant of nationalism.

I Dahrendorf freaks out!

In *The Rise of Regional Europe* (1993) I argued that power was shifting from the traditional nation-state to smaller regional or cultural-national identities, highly-technologised, environment-ally-aware, steered by representatives of Lord Dahrendorf's *Bildungsburgertum*. Then Dahrendorf must have seen *Braveheart*.

The above response is logically wacky. A German ought to be the last to praise 'large' nation-statehood, for God's sake. Wallonia and Catalonia (urban- industrial, though in their time victims of 'large nation-state' fascism) can't be classed with Bosnia and Chechnya (ex-communist peasantry on the Moslem-Christian divide). Yet Dahrendorf has been echoed by well-heeled tellymen like Simon Schama and Niall Ferguson. The mantra that centralisation is *ipso facto* good hovers about in the London and New York media, putting the little platoons again on the defensive.

I argued, in 'Grasping the Thistle' in the BBC's *Scotland 2000* series which helped start the autonomy drive, that growing European integration would make for a 'Europe of the Regions'. Jim Sillars had already reckoned that an autonomous Scotland could thus slip many of its British moorings without awakening the traumas of D.I.V.O.R.C.E, and that our prime alignment seemed to be with the European 'core' and in particular with the 'bourgeois regions' – roughly the representatives of 'Rhenish welfare-capitalism' – which were renewing technical and social structures in a sustainable way, while blurring the frontiers between traditional nation-states. Compare Strasbourg and Freiburg with British towns like Bristol and Southampton or, alas, with anywhere in Scotland. QED.

In the next two decades the imponderables multiplied – not least Sillars himself – and now we have to look at continental developments through the war-shattered prism of a pillaged East, Euro-American diplomatic breakdown and Anglo-American addiction to big stick politics. True, Scotland and Wales got partial autonomy, and Northern Ireland got a very complex settlement, in 1997-8, but were these real concessions by a traditionally overmighty centralist state? Did Britain advance at all towards cooperative federalism? Or, far from central politics being pacific, was military mobilisation the Blairite kneejerk when crises loomed within devolved politics? More ominously, was one European reaction to Balkan instability and the slapdash interventions of Anglo-America, the rise of a regional conservatism, living off economic downturn and anti-refugee emotions, and shifting governments of the centre-right – notably in Austria and Italy – to the right-right?.

One full term of the Scottish parliament has also been a sobering experience. While far from being a failure (in comparison with Westminster or good ol' Bagehotian Cabinet government) it has shown the difficulties of operating with existing party, industrial and administrative structures, and has faced cumulative socio-economic and 'running-in' problems which have reduced its effortlessly superior 'Scots Whitehall' establishment to division if not impotence. Economic parallels with Baden-Württemberg look increasingly shoogly, as we have seen, but there has also been little 'co-operative federalism' and former Scots MPs haven't moved north in droves. An emigré élite ranging from Tony Blair, Robin Cook and Gordon Brown to George Robertson of NATO and Rupert Murdoch of the Powers of Darkness continues, and while the profile of Scots backbench Westminster MPs *as individuals* is subterranean, they remain an important sinister interest keeping Blair in power. The Iraq crisis makes it difficult (though necessary) to analyse where Europe is going; where British development relates (or doesn't relate) to it and where Scotland features in this.

II After the Wall was over

Europe changed profoundly in 2004. The EU now has 25 nations as members, many smaller and poorer than Scotland. Yet it has drifted far from the Europe of the regions-friendly paradigm of 1988-92, and perhaps from the Treaty of Rome ethos, to something closer to the Locarno Pact of the inter-war years: an alliance with the small democracies which are the buffer-zone between the West European 'core' (with or without Britain) and ever-problematic Russia.

The record of the small EU members has been good compared with the UK: 35% richer, enjoying 64% faster growth, smaller deficits and lower unemployment. Since 1988 'Celtic Tiger' Ireland has been there to encourage, if not exactly to be understood. Yet many of Sillars' 1986 arguments have been overtaken by events. What use now are the Common Agricultural and Fisheries policies and the Regional Fund to Scotland? Essentially, Sillars wanted Scotland to play like Ireland, combining participation in Council of Ministers and Commission with national enterprise. But he published *Scotland: the Case for Optimism* in 1986, the year that the Irish economy started to surge forward, going in twelve years from under 60% of British GDP to near parity. It's unlikely that this – driven by a favourable demography, and huge (if generally under-regarded) direct American investment – will recur.

I still stick with my 1987 analysis of the the socio-economic substructures. Eastern central planning was doomed after Chernobyl and the oil price fall, but this took with it, as well as the Comecon market, the huge black economy which involved Ossi factories manufacturing for Wessi concerns and Ossi municipalities burying Wessi rubbish. My Privileg washing machine and spin dryer, and many Ikea goods, were actually Ossi: a low wage input into a high-tech economy, absent from nearly all the liberal accounts – Dahrendorf, Garton Ash, etc. – of reunification.

If Germany stalled after reconstruction, about 1995, this really was what was wrong with it. The ground has mostly been made up: the population of Baden-Württemberg may be up 10% over the decade with ex-Ossis and *Spätaussiedlers* from Russia, but there's been little social discord. Biotech has flourished, along with computerised engineering, environmental engineering; the Mercedes 'A-class' and the 'Smart', the supertrams and ICE trains doing their stuff for not-so-traditional metal-bashing. Housing as a social service has coped with the population expansion – though speculation in it hasn't been there to trigger a high street boom, and the Germans react to a downturn anyway by saving. When Britain's 'incapacitated' (three times the German level) are counted in, unemployment is no worse. But the hiatus has disadvantaged the 'story' of Rhenish capitalism against its 'Anglo-Saxon' competitor.

Will there be an evolutionary or revolutionary outcome to this competition between systems? A reversion towards a regionalised 'core' Europe with strong democratic institutions and civil society, deployed against American globalisation? Or something more fraught? Dahrendorf's panic provides one indicator, but nationalism isn't the only predator. The notion that global US capitalism was benign, and that regionalism could piggy-back on it, looks remote after Enron and WorldCom. But if globalism has called time on Britain, what future for Scotland or Wales? Was the restoration of our 'covenanted sovereignty' an antiquarian enterprise in a post-modern world? Withthe risk of threatening a populist xenophobia, divorced from actual power, but all the more potent for *not* engaging with verifiable data for economic success: *Braveheart* and 'the Serbian way'? There are, as any Scottish Saturday will demonstrate, enough sour old grievances powered by underemployed, drunk young men, to fuel this.

The Thatcher-Major years saw the shameless plundering of the state, a 'victimless crime' because of rising share values. But the failure of Gordon Brown to promote reindustrialisation has been exposed, all the more acute as he has been, in the absence of proto-federal institutions, the determiner of Scottish politics. In 1999 Brown and not Donald Dewar 'took a baseball bat to the SNP' as the *Financial Times* put it. Subsequently he has distanced himself from Jack McConnell, but in the absence of any coherent forward planning – the Monetary Policy Committee of the Bank has little industrial input and no regional remit – the Scottish situation has become infective. Leading sectors which are in constant upheaval, masking substantial and growing social wastage, have now become typical of Britain, accelerated by New Labour spin and turbo-capitalism to the point of impending collapse.

Brown's high-street-led economic growth, touted around Europe as a success, took little notice of a burgeoning trade deficit, a collapsing stock market carrying with it the pensions industry, chaotic financing of the formerly state-run public utilities, and unsustainable household debt. The *quality* of economic growth is being queried even by Prof Ian Oswald and the *Financial Times*, which in 2003 argued that real improvement in living standards *qua* the actual happiness of society hadn't happened since the 1950s.

Despite the PR, 'Old Europe' has done better than Britain infrastructurally, industrially and socially. Baden-Württemberg and Germany have since 1989 coped with population increase and fearsome environmental problems with little political upheaval or growth in support for the far right. On the wider map this has, however, been accompanied by political tendencies which have (with the end of the Cold War and the 'renation-alisation' of fiscal policy in the run-up to the Euro) frustrated and deflected regionalism. With the destabilisation of the Balkans and the accompanying refugee crisis, right-wingers (on closer examination more nationalist than regional) – Haider in Austria, Bossi in North Italy, Blocher in Switzerland, Le Pen in France, the Vlaamse Blok in Flanders, Pim Fortuyn in Holland, the Still-Partei in Hamburg – have been given a boost.

III Our Plutonic Economy?

The challenge to the small states is to re-balance the situation by (a) increasing their socio-economic synergy; (b) cooperating to act as a counter to multinational concerns; (c) playing cultural hardball with 'American' hegemons.

This synergy can promote what Jeremy Rifkin calls the 'third sector' of *spieltrieb* (using the motives of affection, enthusiasm, local loyalty) to regenerate our economy as well as our civil society. But there is also Rifkin's 'fourth sector', in *The Age of Access*, of great and unalterable equality, archaic great-power-nationalism, plus the black economy plus crime.

'Scotland the Bent' (II.v) suggests that this is rapidly gaining on us, in a combination of 'white van man'-type enterprise: the subject of Hans-Magnus Enzensberger's morose essay 'The Italianisation of Europe', outright criminality, and the erosion of the state's monopoly of violence, and 'top-down' corruption through the sheer wealth of individuals unparticular about where their money is coming from

Is this top-down rule-bending, or what we now know about it, accelerating the evolution of a consolidated type of illegality, which might overwhelm civil society? Does the British political élite's involvement with high-level rule-bending – whether in corporate law or consultancy – inhibit it from intervention? Is the European record any better, with Brussels centralisation making matters less transparent and increasing the risks? The Eurostat scandal suggests a quite deliberate attempt to wreck the statistics whose use for comparison ought to be the motor of reform.

If the smaller European states and the regions remain isolated, can we expect more of this? The microstates were unknown to theory until Tom Nairn's 'The Abbot of Unreason and the Lord of Misrule' in *Faces of Nationalism* (1996) in which he saw Andorra, Monaco, and a swathe of British outposts – from the Channel Islands to the Cayman ditto – as the ball-bearings on which international capitalism rolls, maintaining linkages between its unpresentable element and the huge rewards of its bosses. British banking's record in operations such as money-laundering is a very dubious one. And of course businesses which are out to expand – by quite legitimate means – smoking, drinking, gambling and pornography, have knock-on effects on public expenditure. Providing high-cost remedies in health and education increases the returns to PFI concerns.

IV Political and Technical Remedies

Old Europe is circumspect, not unenterprising: the success of its policies can't simply be read off graphs of growth. A society which recycles 50% of its rubbish, repairs footwear and electrics instead of junking them, walks and cycles or goes by bus and train will probably register less in the growth stakes than one which shops its head off, fly-tips its waste, and drives everywhere. The 'Rhenish' regions are still a sober model, with technology and administrative adaptation providing goals that mobilise support and combat multinational interest-groups. The coincidence that both Europe and Scotland need to get their 'machinery of government' straight could prove a useful opportunity for synergy.

Such remedies ought to be in the first line about human rights, infrastructural and environmental policy and, bluntly, ought to be grounded in the Old Europe of pre-1989. Only if this core is functioning efficiently, will it win the confidence on the accession states. If Blair-Brown has a hard landing, Scotland – like Ireland – could play some useful cards to get taken on board.

If Old Europe grows together its own internal regionalism will gain, under the umbrella of general loyalties to European institutions – though the Committee of the Regions has, alas, stayed at the talking shop level. But in France since the Mitterand reforms of 1981 regional power has been growing towards that of the smaller nation-states. A more effective intermediate European authority may be emerging, of the sort detailed in Michael Keating's contribution to the Constitution Unit's *Scottish Independence*, and borne out by the French left's success in the regional elections.

A central factor here is the growing discord within the Scoto-British constitutional settlement. The use of Scottish MPs to support unpopular government policies, plus internal dissidence, has made for party *egoismo*, bureaucratisation and policy stasis, while the new media regulator – OFCOM – has as much regional input as Gordon Brown's Financial Policy Committee, which is zilch. While the slump and turf wars between Executive and Scotland Office has spared the Scottish quangos, now expanding and aligning with new and unfriendly economic pressure-groups, the metropolis becomes even more dynamic.

A Scots or Welsh initiative ought to concentrate on cooperation between Europe's smaller states, both in economic policies – and I would particularly stress combination against monopoly intentions of the great multinationals, by using investor power and selective boycott – and in seeing that Europe's infrastructural net, of education, communications, banking and transport, is dense and co-terminous with its frontiers. A clash between this and the current Atlanticist policy of the British government is pre-programmed.

This raises the issue of the military role of the smaller states, topical because of the division between the USA/Britain and Europe division and the non-functioning of NATO. What happens if the Scottish coalition can't sustain itself? SNP wants the Royal Navy's Trident nuclear-powered-and-armed submarines from the Clyde. Prof William Walker and Dr Malcolm Chalmers of St Andrews and Bradford have argued that without their bases, the expense of relocating the submarines at English ports would force them to revert to

America, leaving Britain a non-nuclear power. But Scotland under a nationalist-led coalition could use Trident as a bargaining-counter, compelling Britain to pool its deterrent with Europe or even, in the last resort, to offer direct Scots-European negotiation over the future of this nuclear arm.

Longer-term, can we negotiate, semi-detached from Europe and the alliances, 'smart' alternative forms of conflict management co-operation between neutralist nations, 'ploughsharing' military budgets to fund high-quality public order interventionism: a combination of weapons control and inspection, low intensity defence and policing operations, and conflict resolution.

Task-groups should have concrete remits. Observe the success of Airbus, and in my own experience the creation of the Open University in Britain in about eighteen months in 1969-71. A similar enterprise – the creation of a European arterial railway system – becomes a lot more than utopian when experts, willing governments and regional politicians are involved. Discuss principles and procedures, yes, but – in Trevithick 200 year – a working iron horse will haul you somewhere.

ii The Media and the Regions

I The Empty Quays

'The author of this novel and all the characters in it are completely fictitious. There is no such place as Manchester.'

Howard Spring's epigraph to his *Shabby Tiger*, written in 1934, seemed appropriate to Manchester in late 2003: not just the trams whining and clanging past the Midland Hotel, back after forty years; and the incredible near-naked girls coasting from club to club (yes, they hadn't changed since Spring's day either).

I was talking immediate media politics: the hypercentralisation of ITV after the Granada-Carlton merger and the market-driven rationalisation of production which closed Granada's Salford Quays studios. Independent television, since 1955 a stimulus to the BBC in terms of regionalism, as well as quality of production, seemed played out. As David Liddiment, late of Channel 4 wrote in the *Guardian,* 'the regional character of ITV is slipping away as talent, money and power continue to be sucked to the centre of the M25'.

. . . or to 'Fucking London' as our Chair, Tony Wilson habitually called it. How much talent, though, has been visible lately in British TV, compared say with 1980? And what remained of the regional-metropolitan feedback/output system in the British media as a whole? Devolution after 1999 was supposed to revitalise the British provinces, but interest in them in the metropolis has sunk to a new low. This is partly political – the choice of a commerce-driven but centrally-regulated régime

(Ofcom) for the media – and partly technical: regional news is now carried by 'London-based' papers but doesn't make their London editions, evicting north-of-the-M25 stories. But it's also due to the provincialisation of London itself.

Looking at 'opinion surveys' in the *Guardian* in November 2003 – on the state visit of President Bush and on university policy, 'opinion' didn't extend as far as Scotland, Wales or Northern Ireland. The *Guardian*, despite its ostensible radicalism (or perhaps because of some old wound of guilt and shame at its desertion of Manchester?) is a peculiarly frequent offender, but this seems typical.

II On the German box

All this stems directly from the absence of 'cooperative federalist' institutions: Blair's shoogly 'reforms' of June 2003, properly derided, being coupled with a failure to decentralise major government bodies. If Germany has its Supreme Court in Karlsruhe, why not have Britain's in York? Nor are we bothered about it, being profoundly ignorant about European media. A recent essay collection for media studies teachers, *Television: Critical Concepts* (Routledge, 2003) had only one piece on regional TV, by Carmelo Garitaonondia, ten years old. Its four books were pervaded by 'soft' subjects – soaps, gender, violence, etc. – and fled from any sort of comprehensive political or civic analysis.

At Manchester, doing my Man-from-Mars act, I thought that the *Sandmännchen*, the little Bündesburger who arrives each night on a spacecraft to put the kids to sleep at 6.55, would be helpful. The first thing he picked up was the link between media regionalisation and (1) governmental/linguistic structures and (2) the public service ethos. TV has to be governmentally-sponsored, licence-fee funded, with only slight commercial input, through adverts and sponsorships, and steered by regional 'arms-length' political bodies. The German public service TV system fundamentally parallels the 1949 *Grundgesetz*, carried only a year before. Its constitution is *Land*-based and its umbrella body the ARD or 'Association of Public Radio-networks of Germany' is like the *Bank deutscher Länder* which became the formidable Bundesbank.

This name emphasises the from-the-ground-up nature of the system. The Zweites Deutsches Fernsehen (ZDF, 1962) is a unitary, federally-established channel based in Mainz, but it gets only 30% of the licence-fee, against 70% for ARD. The Südwest Rundfunk (SWR) is one example: one of ten ARD component channels and a regional federation of stations which was developed as an amalgamated entity in the mid-1990s, finally taking to the air in 1998, with an annual budget of DM 1 billion (£330 million). It was planned by the regional leaders – two SPD (Saarland and Rheinland) and one CDU (Baden-Württemberg) – as an alternative to 'Zwergsender' (dwarf stations) after the impact of the first commercial satellite broadcasters RTL and Sat 1 in 1985. Its constituents Südwestfunk (SWF) and Süddeutscher Rundfunk (SDR) were originally radio systems designed to serve the individual Länder under Allied control – France superintended SWF and the USA SDR – and the TV element came in as one of the eleven regional components of the ARD after 1950. SWR, which transmits to Baden-Württemberg (10.3m); Rheinland-Pfalz (4.0) and Saarland (1.1m) serves a total population of over 15 millions from its main studios in Baden Baden, its headquarters, and Stuttgart, Mainz and Saarbrücken.

Strategy is grounded in the public-interest structure. Its *Rundfunkrat*, or Broadcasting Council of 75 members represents politics, society, academia, and religion. Its executive the *Verwaltungsrat* or Administrative Council supervises its appointee the *Intendant* or Director-General. SWR provides both local and national coverage and also undertakes work for other channels – providing about 17% of programming for ARD – and for its transregional subsidiaries: 3-Sat (German, fairly highbrow), KiKa (a children's channel with no adverts) and the Franco-German cultural channel *Arte*, based in nearby Strasbourg. The major local broadcasts take place from 6-8 every evening, with an hour of magazine followed by Baden-Württemberg News.

There follow through the evening various documentary/ news-magazine/ arts and cabaret programmes, including not a few on Britain, with a bias to the Celtic fringe.

IV The Comedians

Does it work? Criticism comes not only from the commercial satellite channels but from the liberal *Spiegel*, which has a slot on RTL, arguing that audiences are small; standards – particularly in 3-Sat and Arte – too intellectual, or on SWR too plebeian. Indeed, what is the market for 'Mainz wie es singt und lacht, 1977!' meaning ancient jokes from fat men in strange hats who make Andy Stewart look like Noel Coward. Viewers are elderly. Though perhaps ARD/SWR is actually playing smart: the generation who grew up with the box likes to stay with it.

In *Cultural Weapons* (1992) I argued that while German TV seemed a throwback to the pre-'Tonight' BBC: the British 'evening's viewing' was an import from Germany, from the illustrated papers and cabaret of the Weimar period, via *Picture Post* and *Illustrated* as well as Hugh Carleton Greene. This lasted into the 1970s, with Michael Frayn's documentaries on Berlin and Vienna, and Robert Müller's brilliant adaptations of Heinrich Mann's *Man of Straw* and Sybille Bedford's *A Legacy*. British TV in decline is about 'how not to do' things – Simon Schama being prattish about Peter Watkins' still-awesome 'Culloden' – while the Germans are now where we were in the 1970s. With Henrik Breloer's 'The Manns: the Novel of a Century' which ARD produced and transmitted in 2003 – six hours on Thomas and Heinrich Mann and their families, enthralling even *Bild*-readers – they seem to have stayed there.

The ARD federation is driven by an explicit social programme, not by the market. Given Germany's history in the era of film and broadcasting, the reasons for this are obvious. Who was the original spin doctor? How much did Joseph Goebbels learn from the British media? A lot. Germany's adverts may be boring but German politicians are doorstepped all the time. Schröder has the press on him after every Cabinet meeting.

The second shot is always of the reptiles, notebooks and cameras on the go, to remind us that this isn't being fixed.

SWR is only one facet of a decent provincial culture: it has good integration with Ba-Wü's high-quality regional dailies, read by over 60% as against 25% for the tabloid *Bild*. The religious and voluntary sector and what Ralf Dahrendorf calls *Bildungsburgertum* is catered for, and not just in the education or God-slots. In the *Landesschau*, careful archive work and subsequent follow-up discussions about a local spat over a factory closure or a new road really will get an in-depth treatment. This generates regional identity, represents civil society, reports critically inside and outside the German Southwest: a media landscape which advances into a picture of Europe which is civic and regional.

V Sandmännchen sums up

All this is remote from British TV – BBC, commercial or satellite. Will it continue? There are, and will be, problems, exacerbated by the current slump. The public sector ethos, if instructive, is presently awkward. Horns are being drawn in at SWR HQ. On the other hand this Reithianism without the 'man in Whitehall knows best' attitude seems to work. Applied to Scotland it would mean that the Executive's bingeing on the Holyrood parliament would have been nailed years back, its daft plan for a motorway ripping southern Glasgow apart would be getting laldie, and the fact that the real level of Glasgow's unemployment is nearer 30% than 12% would be in the public domain.

The *Sandmännchen* would be puzzled by the hype over the British provincial renaissance, landmarked by cultural overhead capital – the Lowry in which we met, the Newcastle Baltic, etc. This is about remortgage-driven shopping (see Broon, II iii) while high-value-added services (Granada) are, like publishing, schlepped south. If he were a cynical little Sandman, he would see this benefiting not the artist, journalist or viewer, but the lawyers, agents, PR people – the same metropolitan dealers who have enriched themselves at the expense of the consumer, railway-passenger or, in this case, TV viewer. He would be amazed that the crazy costs of London had not, long before now, brought about organisational breakdown, that the Scottish Parliament had not made a bid for media powers an immediate priority.

iii Anglophonia, or the Condition of Britain

I The limits of the civic

Come summer the Scots or Welsh brandish their cans of lager, tattoos and sunburn with the worst. But since about 2000 it has seemed that *Fussballpatriotismus* – once the Tartan-Caliban girning flayed by Tom Nairn – has England in its grip. Above the minor-key politics of dismay trickling from a Whitehall run by damned dangerous North Britons, or the footie money-mill cranked up by Murdoch, there was something even *Daily Record* readers must have registered: a lowest common Britcult squandering integrity and dignity. The civic sense of being responsible for Scotland, or Wales or that provincial Englishness which the Open University represented, was under attack.

'British' no longer seemed to imply Orwellian patriotism but the whispers of a remote North British/North American oligarchy slithering in and out of government, the City, quangoland, edging aside Edmund Burke's 'little platoons' of the neighbourly, the voluntarist and the provincial. Of cooperative federalism there was little sign; devolution had evicted Scotland from the London media.

In Munich the *Suddeutsche Zeitung* runs stories on politics and society in Hamburg or Leipzig – and *three* pages on sport – but Londoners' knowledge of the rest of Britain gets as far as sport, murder, shopping, eating and the annual Edinburgh home-from-home. Should we welcome this 'letting go'? No: we're part of Anglophone culture, and we suffer when it ails.

The university ought to be the power-house of the liberal state. It was in the 1950s and 1960s, with John Smith and Donald Dewar in Glasgow, Malcolm Rifkind, Robin Cook and Gordon Brown in Edinburgh. But now? Edinburgh students were offered free Wagner and Chekhov by the Festival authorities, and a handful turned up. We had no Yeats on stage to shout 'You have disgraced yourselves again!' Student seems to have joined footballer as a Bad Word and I've found that in guest lectures enthusiasm and curiosity come from exchange students, rather than the silent natives and the socialite incomers. The latter 'concentrate on what's needed for a sound 2:1 degree. That gets them a City job,' said an Edinburgh colleague. At worst they seem as a German exchange student put it, 'merry teenagers'. Not my prejudice: the youth of no other European nation speaks its innermost thoughts, so loudly, into its mobile phones on bus and train.

Government ought to promote attitudes which are informed, dignified and tolerant, making their point through style and wit. Patriotism is the desire not to be shamed by one's country. But Britain has become melodrama, with an unending New Labour rhetoric of action and the Conservatives stuck on shriek level the moment Europe is mentioned. Is Britain going the way of Italy under the Christian Democrats – government as a career for sharp lads from the *Mezzogiorno* while the old élite makes money elsewhere? Given the gravity-defying qualities of the economy, flash consumerism appears to pay. MetroBrits are told that they win because they shop their heads off, on phones, fashion, travel, drink 'n footie. Their media – broadsheets and journals as much as tabloids – moulds itself round this, with much 'editorial' matter only a comma or two away from the press release; 'opinion' is 95% London opinion.

The argument might have sharpened up, had the nationalists scored in the Welsh and Scots elections. But war kept New Labour off the Scottish rocks in 2003 – 'stand by our boys' was still worth another ten percentage points to the 'British' parties'– while *Plaid Cymru* was hit by Rhodri Morgan putting 'clear red water' (whatever that was) between Cardiff and

London. The SNP ballsed up its organisation for the second 'list' vote; its reorganisation into a list-based party (like the SPD in Ba-Wü) had been too long delayed. Even so Scots voted for the Greens, independents or Scottish Socialists, and the Lib-Lab coalition majority is down from 16 to 6. The London media dwelt on this for a nanosecond, but even it might wonder what happens if Blair goes out and Brown goes down?

The current 'settlement' depends on the same party ruling in London, Edinburgh, and Cardiff, while Blair's spatchcocked coupling of Whitehall's reserved powers to the persons of Alastair Darling and Peter Hain fits no sort of constitutional theory. Can anyone see Morgan and McConnell obeying Tory-exhumed Secretaries for Wales and Scotland?

**II Ich spreche kein Deutsch. . . No hablo Espanol. . .
Je ne parle pas francais**

As alternative, there's Europe? A long tradition of Scots settlement: Russian architects, poets and admirals, French Marshals, German philosophers. Entrepreneurs everywhere. We like to think we're more European than British. A *Financial Times* survey in 1999 said as much, and you can't throw a stone in Florence without stunning McConnell signing a cooperation agreement. But fewer than a quarter of us can speak any language but our own. When the ambassadors of Germany, France, Spain and Italy reminded us of this in February 2002 in perfect English, they made the point that if we want to learn from Europe, we weren't helping ourselves. Our schoolkids' foreign language capability was down two-thirds on 1980. In tourism – about 750,000 European visitors a year – under 20% of Scottish hotel staff can handle a query in French, far fewer in German or Italian.

In Europe, English may be international, but it makes us complacent. German *Fachsprache* (shop-talk) is how you get through to the man in overalls with the micrometer. You can only know how the economy of computer-assisted engineering works, notably in transport, environmental science and recycling, if you know German. We don't, so we're weak to useless at all three. Look at the technology pages of German provincial newspapers and contrast them with the thinness in this area of British *broadsheets*. Remember that any European can access the *Daily Record* on the net.

We *ought* to be trying to understand such people and processes, but interest in foreign languages and cultures has been for years in free-fall. Tübingen has thirty-odd exchange students from Britain, nearly three hundred from Spain. Language students were once an élite, nowadays many are struggling. Strasbourg University says it gets more problems (drink, sex, pure fecklessness) from British students than from every other national group put together.

Does the answer lie in the schools? Is the basic curriculum too basic, not alluring enough? ('Learn German, chat up Claudia Schiffer.') Are computer studies, with their unfashionable insistence on grammar and system, creaming off the bright kids who once dived into French or German? Is the enthusiasm there? English teachers in Scotland's twinned province, Bavaria, told me that class exchanges, though healthy elsewhere, were almost non-existent with us. The links are weakening. Holidays spent in Italy and in France have been in steady decline. Spain isn't the destination it once was, and army rundown in Germany has added to our weakness in an economic and cultural area where we have some chance of competing effectively.

New technology doesn't help. The Pisa inquiry by the OECD, though not about foreign languages, gave UK education good marks and failed Germany. This was puzzling, as my daughter was well taught in *Grundschule* from 1988-93, and watched enough awful German soaps to make her fluent. But since 1990 BaWü's had nearly two million *spätaussiedler* and satellite TV. Russian programmes are on all hours of the day, so kids don't pick up colloquial German. Because German schools pursue truants – registration means that 'bunking-off' is impossible – failures appear in the record. In the UK up to 20%, our 'functional illiterates', simply vanish. This hidden statistic breeds racism and xenophobia, and we're not immune.

III What to do?

First of all, recognise that a problem can also become an opportunity. Despite our sloth in acquiring languages, foreigners still want to improve their English by coming here. We can use this to build up 'two-way' language acquisition in Scotland through summer schools, in which teachers of English from Europe could get updating courses in Scottish literature, history and politics while giving Scottish schoolkids immersion courses in European languages.

Secondly, twinning between Scots and European communities should junk 'jollies for cooncillors' for swapping individual teachers, small groups of trainees, community bodies, and tourism professionals. We could link this up to courses in language and culture coupled with Open University-style distance-learning.

Thirdly, we must recognise that Scotland isn't a 'young country' and take advantage of the fact. Our over-forties and early-retirees – teachers, technologists and public servants – are folk with the time and the experience to act as mentors in technology and European studies. The person-to-person connections in Scottish Enterprise's 'GlobalScot' programme can be boosted by 'counting in' the French, German and Italians who are 'keen on Scotland'; the reservoir of goodwill is immense if we can use the magic words to unlock it. And these aren't always English words.

iv Bookfloggers and branders: selling Scotland or finding partners

I Lions' den

Sonia Orwell, though a stunner, wasn't a very nice person. For little magazines in the 1940s, trying to balance printers' bills and subscriptions, a quick-release mechanism was 'Send Sonia round to seduce them'. Perhaps a model for Anthony Powell's superbitch Pamela Widmerpool, she nonetheless helped John Calder to set up the Edinburgh Writer's Conference in 1962, where old monsters like Henry Miller and Hugh MacDiarmid, penurious but impenitent, did their stuff.

George Orwell, on his centenary, was a featured writer at the Edinburgh's Bookfest. Would he have liked it? Not over-impressed by London's 'lousy little literary lions', my hunch is that he would have shunned Charlotte Square like the plague, and in a *Scotsman* piece I guessed that its outcome would have about as much to do with the 'unwelcome guerilla's' concern with real political community, as that other litfest, Hay-on-Wye, has to do with Wales.

Books are subversive, which Orwell relished. But what happens when literature stops being a critique of the industrial society that accompanied the rise of the novel, and becomes a service-industry commodity, inducing that sense of despair one has in the big booksheds, whose vastness and vacuity say interior décor not intellect?

Ray Bradbury and Francois Truffaut knew this. It's almost impossible to watch *Fahrenheit 451* without blubbing, when the refugees from a philistine video-society *become* books by memorising them: 'I'm *The Master of Ballantrae*', he's *The Brothers Karamazov*.'

II Whose literature?

I have taken Bookfest's geld and enjoyed my exhibition bouts with Allan Massie before a raging mob from Jenners' tearoom. I don't enjoy biting hands that feed, and as a historian with a day job and English publishers, I can think of many Scots colleagues who ought to have priority over me. But when Edinburgh Book Festival director Catherine Lockerbie praised 'an invasion of American writers' I thought 'Oceania'. Hypercapitalism, as Orwell himself admitted, could produce *1984* on its own, being as keen as Ingsoc about eliminating unhelpful history. Or awkward subjects like the culture of Old Europe. Would the Charlotte Square folk discuss Enzensberger's new poems? Jurgen Habermas' and Umberto Eco's critique of American cultural imperialism? Would Europe's senior political man-of-letters, ex-President Havel, get grilled about how it was for him?

What we got was Big Apple writ global: not something that requires our charity, rather the reverse. Simon Schama's ghastly *History of Britain South of the M25* was beamed out by the national broadcaster, and – more formidable because its presenter at least attempted a logical narrative – Niall Ferguson's *Empire*. Both are now New York academics, and you bet that their target isn't five million Scots. The casualties *are* the 'little platoons' – the vital culture of local literary societies, community writers' groups, small publishers – squeezed by the megaprints and megastores, until they resemble Truffaut's refugees.

Scotland is *here*, but what is Bookfest doing for it? For our non-existent national theatre, and our all-too-salient Holyrood (which might just redeem itself as a cultural powerhouse)? For our films that get praised but don't get screened? For our imperilled literary journals? For our sad, dope-and-booze-threatened younger generation? Bluntly comes the answer: bring 'Sex and the City's' Candice Bushnell, 'overpaid, oversexed, over here', to the place with the worst sexual health in Europe! Give us Irvine Welsh, the Enid Blyton of *Porno*!

Harry Potter (I've read enough not to get hooked) originated in Edinburgh, and was subsidised by the Scottish Arts Council. But what of this dividend came back to us from Carlyle's 'huge, subterranean puffing bellows' of the London book trade? Bugger all. Is this a subject for debate? Surprise me.

Yes, there were some Scots moments, when the Injuns got to sell blankets on the fringe of the reservation. (Allow them to run a casino? Don't joke.) Even so, in the 2003 programme the forum on Scottish publishing cancelled out Carol Craig on Scottish psychology, like the only cars on a Highland road managing to crash into each other.

III Our good books

Bookfest is a public interest operation. Good. But it ought to be there to criticise, to be against the big guys, and to interrogate the motives of all culture-marketing colossi. The Edinburgh Film and TV Fest is not a good role-model. Grabs headlines, sure, but look at the state of British broadcasting, properly rubbished by Richard Hoggart in a recent *Guardian*. We ought to be planning our resources. Scots bookselling may be down the drain, but we still have publishers who can compete. The big Constance conference in 2003 on Walter Scott depended on Edinburgh University Press's scholarly editions. Birlinn and Tuckwell published Michael Fry's *Scottish Empire* and (for all my frequent compulsions to lamp Fry for one reason or another) this was an achievement which knocked Schama-Ferguson into a cocked hat. When I wrote my transport polemic *Deep-Fried Hillman Imp* two years ago Derek Rodger of Argyll printed it – in Scotland – at a reasonable price. It paid its way and – thank you Tommy Sheridan! – helped influence debate during the election. Were London publishers interested in a British critique? Don't ask.

All this is nationalism? Yes and it damn well should be, because the nation is a community, the health of all of whose members matters, and to which a bland transnational commercialism makes no contribution. The way Bookfest is going reminds one of Alasdair Gray's 'Institute' in *Lanark*, isolated from the world, and living off its casualties.

Ralph Vaughan Williams, perhaps the greatest of English composers, said that without nationalism there could be no healthy internationalism. RVW was no fogey but a socialist and European federalist. In literature, we can aim for his standards. If we don't, we get Andrew Lloyd Webber.

IV Branded to death?

PR is to the 'Scotland Abroad' scene what Hitler is to the History Channel. A long-term resident, and more of a problem than a cure. Indeed, finding one's way through the thicket of smiley stories to some sort of fact is difficult. We earn £4 billion a year from tourism (VisitScotland): hooray! We earned in 2002 10% less from it than in 2001 (Index of Scottish Production): huh! We are spending a third more abroad than we're taking in, a dead cert if we have a strong pound. £3.5 billion may be going out against £2.5 billion coming in. This matches the UK stats and has the ring of truth.

We welcome an annual 300k visitors from Germany and a like number from France (American numbers are despite all the Tartan flapdoodle low and will fall with the $, let alone the effects of 9/11). All credit to the Europeans – 11% of the total visiting Britain – for getting past the tacky swamp of London (second rate waxwork show, display of Japanese neon ads, Europe's most boring palace) where, for too many, the first expensive, discouraging, visit is the last.

But are we encouraging our continental guests? There are well-produced brochures from VisitScotland, and I've counted up to 15 guidebooks in German, but little evidence of Scottish initiatives, although the biggest single group using the Zecbrugge-Rosyth ferry are German. No ads in *Stern*, *Spiegel* or *Zeit*, no brochures in the *ICE* trains and when Germans get here, few who can speak their language. The Americans were never big spenders, but the 'revoluzzers' of 1968 are all now grandparents: Europe's most secure generation, time on their hands and good for another twenty years, are oozing money. They want culture, history, good food and landscape and will pay for it. They don't want MTV screamers, malls, drunk yoof, Old Firm dimwits, and noise. If we want them as partners, they'll play.

V With Friends like that. . .

In the midst of this is the Scottish Executive's Friends of Scotland, spelt 'chocolate teapot'. I was asked to join by Ambassador Paul Lever in 2002. £326,000 was spent up to April 2003: £700-odd per Friend, which has brought me 'Update', an online version of the scan-and-bin mags you get on the train, a book of stamps and a mouse-mat. This best laid plan has gone seriously agley. The cash could be put to better use.

The private sector *per se* isn't an answer. PR folk would crawl naked over red-hot coals for a London postcode, making the BBC look like a paragon of decentralisation: since 1999 London media has done little for the Thule north of the Chilterns, and cared less. Yet we have abundant resources made up from the local, the enthusiasts, the semi-retired, and the networks they've built up. Titter ye not, MSPs. Without the likes of Robert Grieve, Paul Scott, Jim Ross and Kenyon Wright, you would not exist.

In autumn 2002 I took part in Cromarty's Hugh Miller Bicentenary bash. This was stylish, intellectually top-notch, moving and great fun, holding its own against Germany's 'Goethe 250' in 1999. It was almost completely amateur-run by all sorts of Scots by birth and choice, and made this exile deeply proud of the place – quite different from the grotesque MTV awards, where national feeling was fondled by some pop careerist mouthing 'Flower of Scotland' for the teenies, and much money was lost.

VI Representation

So, what about a team using FoS funding to set up an independent consortium involving the universities, heritage organisations, local arts bodies, churches, etc., to provide our voluntary organisations with high-quality skills and backup, and a programme to link with European environmental or cultural groups as partners, not as targets. An arms-length task-force could compete with government bodies and the British Council (whose grip has faltered lately) for contracts to represent Scotland abroad. Such competition would keep both up to scratch, furthering direct partnerships in technology, education, social work, offering scholarships and work experience . . . not to speak of shaming our fat-cat bankers, retailers and brewers into doing something for our environment and culture.

Partnership can feed the demand that clearly exists for summer schools – look at the Irish successes: Yeats, Joyce, Carleton, Hewitt, Merriman – the marketing of books and crafts, the organisation of specialist holidays. It can remedy the deficit that the *Herald* noted in quality Scottish books at historic sites. More, it can help create the partnerships which alone can repair our imperilled infrastructure, as continental industrial regions are desperate to provide things like railway, recycling and power-generation equipment, which we no longer do. We can only co-opt them by winning them over.

Our thing in our favour may be the 'Celtic Fridge' effect. *Hitze* in Europe – global warming turning the Mediterranean sun into a blowlamp – is only hot weather here. Could Scotland become not just somewhere to flee to in summer but maybe a salvation for threatened European holiday firms – two-thirds of Swiss ski resorts may close by 2020 – looking for investment alternatives.

Where? Take the Millenium Canals. These could rival Ireland's money-spinner, the Shannon, with the techno-bonus of the Falkirk Wheel. Yet I walked the towpath recently from Clydebank to Bowling, without seeing a boat, or any prospect of the marinas, moorings and the sort of canalside development that you get in Birmingham or Rochdale. We have folk who can market such resources – from the Cromarty Arts Trust to the volunteers of the Scottish Railway Preservation Society. They aren't bureaucrats, and they aren't media. It's time to give them their chance, and FoS's money, before we end up branded to death.

IV. Strategies
i The Economics of Everyday

'You know, the French haven't got a word for entrepreneur.' President George W. Bush

'If they devolve enterprise to local firms, then the folk running things in Buckhaven will be the bookies'. John Milne's gift for the one-liner makes, as ever, a good point. 'Enterprise culture' has become a mantra of our times, to be conveyed to the tinies along with their lego-bricks. I seem to get a mail about this most weeks from GlobalScot. In due course we'll hear in the *Daily Record* of some kid creating a micro-Walmart to flog his schoolmates crisps and fizzy drinks. Do we applaud?

We might if he/she were flogging salads grown in the school greenhouse, and we might applaud even more if he/she persuaded their schoolmates to finance the business by buying shares out of cash saved by ditching designer sportswear. I've the suspicion the some of our role-models – the Tom Hunters and Michelle Mones – might at this stage become less enthusiastic. Still, I suggest some fields in which 'enterprise', 'delivery', etc., can meet the goals of the good society.

I Trashing it

Scotland has the world's worst recycling record. Affluent first world countries work hard at processing, recycling or avoiding their waste. In very poor third world countries you'll always find someone dealing in empty bottles or cardboard or plastic bags. The sort of throwaway society we have, buying cheaply and ditching rather than repairing, is the creation of the B-division of the first world. In Tübingen less than 50% of our junk is *Restmüll*: papers and packing are collected once a month, with less frequent collections of dangerous refuse – from turpentine to batteries – garden rubbish, 'elektroschrott' (computers, TVs). On *Sperrmülltag* everything from three-piece suites to dish-dryers is left out on the pavement, for the general public to help itself, and what remains goes to the council: either sold off or (if suitable) burned in a generator.

Recycling is never going to make a profit, but not to do it is morally and increasingly politically impossible. Europe won't let us get away with it. But using expensive equipment and manpower to shift low value stuff is a waste of money. The German system isn't perfect: it actually works by the charges made for *Restmüll*. Once paper, plastic, compost is removed, I pay about €140 annually to be rid of a couple of sacks! The cash could be better spent than on having big trucks running about the place, so why not develop local heating/power systems (our university generator is 90% efficient, against 37% efficiency at Torness). These could be operated by heat engines that use, for example, briquettes made from paper, picked up by a local truck system, compressed by small-scale equipment, and used in a clean-burn process. For plastic, again, why not local schemes which convert polyurethane foam into insulation? And we surely still have the technology (at Moss Morran and Grangemouth) to convert plastics back into oil or gas for use as fuel?

Again you can't get far along this track without becoming dependent on technology, and this can probably only be provided on the scale we need by inter-region agreements. But the frictional costs of this can be lessened by integrating such projects with the educational system. Integration of the 'candidate countries' with their pretty solid Soviet-era engineering skills could give a timely bonus here, with the hi-tech contribution coming from Western Europe and Japan.

II Delivering it

At Tübingen we have a market in the town's squares four times a week. Get there early and you can scoot round the stalls and fill up the shopper in twenty minutes with meat, fish, vegetables and fruit, cheese, pasta. All right, we have just about the most beautiful town square in Europe, but the friendliness, the encounters with traders whom you've known for years, and whom you trust, sets you up for the day. And precious little of the food on offer will do you any harm.

Cut to Scotland where not a week goes by without the announcement of some 'mammoth retail development' – Asda, Sainsburys, Safeway, etc. – usually accompanied by much brouhaha about the creation of hundreds, thousands of jobs. This usually comes from the PR folk, endorsed by such credulous cooncillors as come to hand, and is big-scale baloney. Malls aren't in the business of job-creation, but of running a lean retail-machine, preferably en route to a local monopoly. They will certainly provide part-time jobs, but will replace with national or even international linkages a supply-side which was formerly local. The high-value-added bits of accounting, banking and transport services will vanish. And are standards necessarily any better?

The case of 'Maggot Pete' who marketed condemned meat (too foul even for pet-food) for years showed that a crook with enough resources and brass neck could bribe public health officials and win a way through to the most respectable food chains. And he's not the last, as 'best before' has become yet another modern icon to discover the joys of flexibility.

The weekly trip to the mall seems socially self-destructive. The long distances travelled to, and then within, the shed, the traffic congestion around the entrance, the buying of unnecessary bargains, the lack of human contact with the staff. Compared with Tübingen market this is a chore; it can also take a surprisingly long time. And look what it does to your local high street! Charity shops, estate agents, boozers, places for idle yoof to make pests of themselves.

Your supermarket bill: how much of this stuff do you need to buy personally? Bottled water (then again, why?), flour, margarine, milk, yoghurt, beer, toilet paper, kitchen roll, freezer bags, probably three-quarters of it, by weight, could be ordered and delivered, sight unseen. For 'quality shopping' – ghastly phrase – you could go downtown in the bus with your basket. The obvious problem is that there has to be someone at home to deliver to. Unlikely these days. So why not have delivery to your nearest corner shop, who can either keep it for you or deliver when you get home – thus keeping him/her in business as well? All of this requires a bit of planning, but it is something that can be done locally. It should also increase the number of 'real' jobs created.

Local shopping or delivery is also essential to the growing number of us who're elderly, for whom the shop is a necessary place to go to gossip, to check in, prove that you're alive. Going to the post-office to collect your pension is one of the things that brings old folk together: now all this is to be replaced by transfers which will cut the number of branches, baffle the elderly, and further emaciate the high streets.

III Recovery and Dignity

It was they who had passed
The ruined temple outside, whose eyes
Wept pus, whose back was higher
Than his head, whose lopsided mouth
Said Grazie in a voice as sweet
As a child's when she speaks to her mother
Or a bird's when it spoke
To St Francis.

Norman MacCaig, 'Assisi'

A problematic 250,000 Scots have been damaged by drink or drugs, a proportion probably unparalleled elsewhere in Europe. If the drastic steps outlined in Scotland the Bent are taken to end the druggy economy, these fellow-citizens will have to be rehabilitated, something that our existing institutions have failed to do. We all know the shambling husks on the park benches. But for many of them recovery – if attempted – has been as lonely as the descent into addiction.

In Germany the *Obdachlose* (houseless) are of various sorts, but there are quite large numbers of well-organised itinerants, usually with a drink problem, who manage to achieve at least some kind of corporate survival. In Tübingen the 'Berber' got cash and timber from the town to build themselves a stockade for their tents, with water and toilets. Quite spontaneously, a group of drunks which had been living under a bridge in Leipzig, started to collect for Bosnian refugees. They filled up a van with medicine and toys for the kids and, for a time, became heroes. Solidarity and activity could spring them from a cycle of despair: something that can be used to reintegrate the excluded in society by giving responsibility for self-organisation in areas like environmental improvement, horticulture, recycling, delivery and aid to the elderly. It also involves careful supervision and dedication on the part of officials detailed with this work. But in connection with some of the enterprises outlined above, it could pay off.

If we do establish localised power-generation, the fuel has to be gathered and processed, and the surplus heat will facilitate greenhouses and propagators: an alternative 'green' food source yielding a range of transitional jobs for those re-entering society. But for this to succeed we need forms of marketing which are different from the malls and megastores.

This is where civilian service could be vital, and could also be used to help finance higher education. National service was boring and humiliating, and never awoke much loyalty to the state, but civilian service can impress on young people that they must pay for their privileges, besides giving practical training to balance the theory of higher education. As to finance, this should be voluntary as much as state-derived, through tax-breaks which encourage firms to create, individually or jointly, beneficial trust organisations. The banks and bank bosses are deriving huge profits from our debt culture; the brewers' lust for profit has led them to wind down Scottish production, and put a generation at risk by encouraging an unrelenting booze culture. They too should be granted the opportunity to repent and reconstruct, by those means – and this means you Moir Lockhart, Sandy Crombie, Angus Grossart, Fred Goodwin, Brian Soutar, Peter Burt – the example of the likes of George Soros ought to matter to you. Remind yourselves of the use you made of Andrew Carnegie's libraries, and of that old rascal-turned-saint's line 'The man who dies rich, dies disgraced'.

IV God stand up for Anoraks!

In the 1960s I helped set up the Scottish Railway Preservation Society and what became the Scottish Public Transport Association, and worked on the Festiniog Railway, so I was a right anorak and thus an object of pity. I suppose I can answer back that I'm still around and active when most of my more hedonistic contemporaries are not, and when the lads 'n ladettes of more recent times have fallen into well-merited oblivion. So that settles that. No it doesn't, for looming on the plateau above Porthmadog, is the vast bulk of the Trawsfynydd nuclear reactor, in service from 1965 to 1996, and presently being dismantled. The core will be sizzling for the next 30,000 years or so, but the generator is finished, along with 600 or so local jobs.

As a platelayer on the Festiniog when this folly was rising, I have seen it all, and been justified while the Great and Good, and sundry well-heeled consultants made idiots of themselves. Protesting against rail closures, motorways, nuclear stations and shopping malls, and trying to conserve the local and traditional was old hat. It was also right.

My friend Iain McLean, Professor of Politics at Oxford, is presently causing grief to McConnell because he wants to sort out the Barnett formula in the interests of the English regions. McLean, a companion on various mildly strenuous Munros in the mid-1960s, seemed to have an almost unerring eye for the right cause at the wrong time. He did an undergraduate thesis on Ulster politics and gave the subject up, in 1967. He did a

BPhil on Scottish nationalism, and announced it as exploded, in 1968. His DPhil in 1971, debunking (very convincingly) the Red Clyde myth, was unfortunate in coinciding with the great days of Jimmy Reid and Jimmy Airlie. He was an enthusiast for the SDP in 1981. But at the same time Anorak McLean helped set up the Welshpool and Llanfair Railway on the marches of Wales, a boon and a blessing to that region, and while Labour Finance Convener of Tyne and Wear Council in the 1970s, got through the Tyneside Metro, the precursor of the light railways which can (given a chance) now save our cities.

Main-line McLean, in other words, has been as hit or miss as your man at pressing the button of relevance (I can't make head or tail of him on games theory or public choice, but his history of the Aberfan tragedy and its shameful cover-up is stunning). Branch-line McLean came out right all the way through, and the combination of both is formidable. As good an argument as you can get for the *spieltrieb* that we need, the sort of thing that Robert Putnam and Jeremy Rifkin try to boost, and Pat Kane and his www.theplayethic.com project is digitalising. Enthusiasm doesn't detract from expertise, it enhances it. So, Jack, be afraid, be very afraid. . . or get it on your side.

V The Curse of Gnome. . . or a Philosophy of Society

In 1999, wanting to commemorate the opening of our Parliament, Peter Jones of the *Economist* and I published *The Road to Home Rule*, a record of the saga, with pictures and conversations. STV showed interest, and talked of up to three documentary films to launch it. We didn't expect to make a lot, and wanted much of what transpired to go into a 'Tom Johnston Trust' to expand (initiate?) political and civic education in Scottish schools. STV then fell silent. Their cash went, instead, to buying over Chris Evans' outfit Ginger Productions for £250 million. Then the Curse of Gnome fell on them: the lolly bought Evans the biggest carry-out in British media history and most of their investment went down the pan. Andrew Flanagan's vision of media hegemony turned into a car-boot sale of SMG's assets.

Of Jones and Harvie's civic goals, nothing survived, but all guilt-ridden millionaires, take note. I recount this sorry tale (a) to put the boot in, and (b) to make the point that devotion to the bottom line doesn't pass, or even start, as a philosophy of life, least of all the sort that we want to bequeath to our children. And philosophies of life have always been important in Scottish *academe*.

In 1961, the year before I went to Edinburgh University, George Davie published his *Democratic Intellect*, on the glories of the Victorian Scots universities with their philosophic first year, whose intake was, if anything, more democratic than today's; when students would assess the papers of their fellows, and formal teaching was reinforced by debates and political clubs. Something of the sort survived into my time. I'm grateful for it, and I've tried to replicate it in my own teaching, in making the students, as much as possible, responsible for organising our two-hour seminars. (You can learn more about this by accessing the Tübingen Landeskunde website www.intelligent-mr-toad.de)

I think it works. I also think it's applicable to the reorganisation of our higher education system, to rescue it from overspecialisation and, along with civilian service, to give students a sense of the ways in which society interpenetrates with, and relies on, their professional work. Bluntly, it doesn't matter much whether students turn up at lectures – we had no control over this at the Open University – as long as they read (or watch or listen) and have a dialogue with a responsible teacher individually or in flexibly-organised seminars.

Thomas Carlyle said that Edinburgh University in the 1810s was dreadful but that no place with a good library could be a total disaster, and the MAs who were Davie's heroes had the freedom as *Privatdozents* to take students as private pupils. Combining anoraks and literati, the sort of university I'd like would have its classes all over the central belt in a Faculty of Scotland, and the students would use their cheap seasons (travel costs my lot €70 a year) to move from one institution to another, by train or tram, naturally. If we create the German post of *Wissenschaftlicher Hilfskraft* (scientific assistant) who earns about €500 a month for secretarial/ organisational work, while acting as a sort of academic apprentice, we will enhance academic output and put more students through the system. This may cramp the style of 'merry teenagers' who just wanna have fun. Tough.

ii Can we afford Scotland?

I Barnett and the balance of payments

First of all the Balance of Payments. Seen from the south, most recently by the aforesaid Iain McLean, Jocks are overrepresented at Westminster and get 20% more out of the public funds than they should.

Things aren't quite as simple as that. If Scotland has 10% more productivity in manufacturing than the English, exports 30% more – a higher per capita figure than the Japanese – and possesses most of West Europe's oil and gas reserves, how come it's a subsidy junkie? Prof Clive Lee, in *Scotland in the United Kingdom* argues that independence is an uneconomic proposition, even with 90% of oil revenues. But taxation has a geography, and Lee has to admit that his taxation pattern is British, but his social expenditure is Scottish. The Barnett Formula of 1978 makes Scotland a limited contributor but demanding beneficiary. But what actually is going south?

Lee tells us to beware George Rosie and Arnold Kemp, who saw public expenditure and mortgage tax relief pumping cash into the English south-east, but say nothing about the billions going on London infrastructure. Reckoning public transport schemes alone, I stopped counting at £20 billion. . .

Lee admits that much wealth generated in Scotland shows up as London tax income, and that takeovers have hit the Scottish financial sector: 'merchant banks lost accounts as the result of the takeover of Scottish companies and the relocation of their headquarters . . .' But he doesn't go into the implications of the fact that, between 1985 and 1986 *alone*, £2.4 billion out of £4.7 billion of Scottish manufacturing capital went south. Such issues demand a new input-output model of the Scottish economy, of the 1976 sort, but there's no sign of it.

II Private profit, public costs

There is a further implication. Asked about policies for assisting small businesses, the cookery entrepreneur Prue Leith said that the most useful thing would be more money for redundancy payments. The economics of modern manufacturing are: new technology equals bigger profits equals smaller labour force.

Consider ScotWidget, taken over by British Widgets. British Widgets are nice guys, put new technology in their SW plant, though a bit of rationalisation is involved, and 100 out of the 400 SW employees are declared redundant. British Widgets do well, so profits go south to London and (if taxed: most big firms are pretty streetwise and many multinationals are utterly elusive) figure as UK, not Scottish, taxation income. The redundant workers soak up social security and get ill more often; kids can't get jobs, so stay longer in school or college. Growth in Scottish productivity actually increases public sector expenditure in Scotland. McLean and Lee don't go into this at all.

Remember that Barnett dates from 1978 when the first oil was pumped ashore. All 'British' parties had promised an 'oil fund' for Scotland, to stop the SNP running off with it. Oil duly bankrolled Mrs Thatcher, and everyone forgot about any fund. But this makes Barnett, and any public expenditure surplus accruing therefrom, look less like a dole and more like a contract. Oil again emphasises how private benefits become public costs. Exploitation swallowed £60 billion in investment between 1969 and 1994; creating perhaps a total of 130,000 jobs, but also devastating many local firms: look at the North-East. If Barnett kept the UK together, we are still forking out for the social and infrastructural costs created by such a high-productivity industry, without having any control over it.

McLean doesn't mention oil. Lee plays it down. It might make a difference; but not enough, since the shortfall in taxation income is bigger than the current oil tax proceeds of £1.6 billion: choices 'painful in the extreme' would still have to be made in cutting expenditure.

But oil prices have since soared and the stuff will be around, if not for ever, then for long enough, prompting the question why does the UK get such a miserable income from it? At maximum output in the later 1990s less than half the public dividend from oil that Norway – pulling in £5 billion – got. Half of this was in tax and royalties, and the other half from the country's oil-exploiting public enterprises.

Gordon Brown in *The Red Paper on Scotland* demanded: 'Nationalisation of all offshore oil and gas industry (and) the proceeds of oil . . . transferred into a regional development fund.' And then forgot about it, although Norwegian social democracy pulled in the sort of income that Tony Benn's British National Oil Corporation would have secured. Will Hutton reckoned that a return to the 1987 regime could screw a further £3 billion out of the multis. And who am I to disagree with precepting a chunk of this for Scottish purposes? Otherwise, Scottish 'success' in oil leads to another national deficit, to be followed by microelectronics with (for all the impact of Scottish Enterprise's Locate in Scotland campaign) low-cost professionals and high-cost infrastructure used as the bait for multinationals.

The Barnett stushie shows up the lack of Labour thought about how Scotland can be retained in the UK by means short of federalism. The most logical financial order would be to follow the German system whereby tax is raised by councils, and at each level appropriate percentages for local expenditure, Scottish expenditure, and UK expenditure are precepted, with an Equalisation Board making such topping-up transfers as are necessary.

III Neo-classical endogenous misbehaviour

They laughed when Gordon Brown spouted neo-classical endogenous growth theory. They're not laughing now. The lumbering formula seemed in 1994 to imply regional renewal, yet what it meant was hypermarketism: the absence of solidarism, within society, within the family, within personal relationships. Hence the multiplication of households, which drove up the price of housing, and the remortgaging which supplied the resources to factor this into private transport and retailing. Result: market-driven economic growth or retail therapy? The bailiffs won't be particular.

The costs of this were: the relative disadvantage of manufacturing, the public sector, the health service, the care of the elderly, and the environment. The privatisation of the railways was attributed to John Major, but in fact it conformed to the Brownite paradigm: instead of a planned corporate provision of infrastructure, a landscape of neo-classical endogenous bargaining was created which by raising the costs of the system from £2million to £10 million annually, injected this much into national 'growth'. The City of London, shovelling the billions and seeing tidy sums sticking to its shovels, wasn't going to complain.

IV A philosophy of nationalism

The other element is the old call of '*la Patrie en danger*'; of Sir David Lindsay's *Three Estates*, of Burns's 'Twa Dogs', of Davie's *Democratic Intellect*. By now, I hope, you'll see where *Mending Scotland*'s argument has been heading. Our post-modern age has become 'post-historical', in that the data out of which we construct our analyses have been distorted by being 'politicised'.

The insecurity which has migrated from our old heavy industries and their once-organised working class has acted on an equally-insecure middle class, particularly its younger members. Surviving in such circumstances is eroding the corporate identity that the nation ought to provide.

The Scots problem is basically that of retaining social equilibrium in a trans-national Europe. This involves building up new and hard-and fast interregional partnerships, but is complicated by its intersection with a generational crisis: a young post-professional class now on the *qui vive*. Our property-powered pseudo-growth has accelerated at their expense: they cannot afford the 'starter homes' which Irvine Welsh's junkies mocked. Hence they've become the 'useful idiots' of consumerism. The security of their parent's generation seems a pretty hopeless prospect, and a *mittelstand-kultur* which favours small businesses has rarely got beyond rhetoric, hence the charm of 'living for the day' and the evolution of types of hedonism or semi-religious belief that comfort this essentially nihilistic outlook: the reversal to a mythic religion of 'celebrity' temporary kings out of J.G. Frazer, of ritual dancing and determined drinking.

This is a sort of Popperian 'return to the tribe' rather than the *Spieltrieb* that Pat Kane wants us (quite sensibly) to cultivate. But it has to make a living, and in the circumstances it turns on its colleagues, like one of Konrad Lorenz's geese. More blatantly than ever before, we see an autistic individualism destroying the state. 'Scotland the bent' exists because, in general terms, there is no foundation any longer for the rule of law, save that of commercial convenience.

So: can Scotland survive? Yes, but only with difficulty, though that difficulty simply parallels more general human dilemmas which we'll sooner or later have to come to terms with. We have to tackle our problems by looking simultaneously in two directions: first at the way in which international and inter-regional relations are moving; and second at potential and actual dysfunctions within our society, to see where synergies in it can be recreated. Our episode of autonomy has made these pretty clear. We now have to go to work.

In the great mural of 'The Benefits of Good Government' in Sienna's town hall, a bare-breasted angel hovers between the town wall and the vineyards, fields and woods of its contado. She holds a small gallows with a hanging man: the symbol of justice and the state's monopoly of force. Today she'd look like a symbol of the *Sun*. But nothing has changed: law still has to be imposed.

The 'global order' isn't an order because capitalism isn't static and concerned with eternal values, but congenitally mobile and innovative. Its outcomes are not universally positive, just as in the past when Scottish affluence was bought through the despoliation of other peoples by the drink and drugs which we sold them. As ever, there will be plenty of Scots to defend this, most notably Rupert Murdoch, whose own bed-hopping career – Australian newspaper dynast, Scots Catholic, Chinese Communist boss's daughter – seems instructive.

Finding a philosophy for twenty-first century Scotland is a difficult task. Some areas of it will have to be authoritarian and strictly-policed. If our drug problem is to be overcome, the national control of hard drugs and the supervision and rehabilitation of their victims must be state-driven. In other areas what we need is the immediacy of a market response, and the dismantling of layers of bureaucratic jobsworths. But we've been around long enough to learn that the jobsworths aren't confined to the public sector, that the sort of gargantuan capitalism that runs our lives has an interest in building up such cadres which (almost) parallels its executives' desire for the bonuses which will as soon as possible set them on the Muirfield fairway. It uses its media power to rubbish the alternatives. I have tried, by comparison between my two worlds, to explain what these are and where they exist.

I set out to write this book for two reasons: to experiment with a new type of teaching book, which combined the convenience of good ol' Gutenberg with accessing material through new technology. Both sorts of media, in conventional form, have big problems. The academic book has become a hermetic and expensive discourse – a toll to be paid to appease the Research Assessment Exercise – the 'trade book' a commodity where what matters isn't sense but sales.

That our most popular historian is Niall Ferguson, a man

who is to history what Mel Gibson is to religion, says it all. From the web flows unsorted stimuli of all sorts, a sea of information in which we drown. So a pocket guide, a Baedeker of Cyberland, is more important than ever. The links are available which at least set out my course across this ocean of fact; you're welcome to follow, or to strike out on your own, but at least there's an argument that you can take issue with. All the above developments mean that this flexibility will urgently be needed.

Further Reading and Websites

Read more about it!
If you follow up the various chapters of *Mending Scotland* in
www.intelligent-mr-toad.de you'll find out how I constructed
the arguments in them. I hope that this will lead you to do this
for yourself (for general study details see *The Bumper Book of
British Landeskunde* (2004) in <toad>.

My chapter on 'Referendum to Millenium' (1978-2000) pp. 494-
531 of RAB Houston and W W J Knox *The New Penguin History of
Scotland* (Harmonsworth: Penguin Books, 2002) has acted as a
general background. This in turn drew on three main feedstocks:

(1) a press-cutting collection
which I've built up since 1990, under main sections: UK,
Scotland, Celtic Britain, Germany, Europe, World, Media,
Transport. The Scottish section of this, drawn from the *Herald*,
Scotsman, *Times*, *Guardian* and *Sunday Herald*, *Financial Times*,
Scotland on Sunday, *Observer* is divided into (a) society, (b)
economics, (c) oil, (d) politics. It has tended to concentrated on
survey articles, in which the *Financial Times* is particularly rich.

(2) the Web
Usually accessed through Google, this responds pretty efficiently
if asked the right questions. I have included details of a few key
sites but these can frequently change. More and more web
archives are being commercialised, with the Murdoch press in

the foreground and the *Scotsman* heading in that direction. The *Guardian* www.newsunlimited.co.uk remains free, and the BBC www.bbc.co.uk and www.scottish.parliament.uk open out the public service and official statistics landscape in Scotland. Websites which enable cross-Europe comparisons to be made seem absent. Doubtless they'll evolve, but I see this initiative coming from Europe, not from the UK where the websites of banks, transport companies, etc. seem constructed to project an image and win custom, not to open themselves to analysis. Mans native Scots websites are sadly primitive: www.bahn.de will give you a timetable for Motherwell-Edinburgh far faster than www.scotrail.co.uk!

(3) Books
Of limited value for the bang-up-to-date, given the time taken to move from manuscript to print. Still, the book can still convince through selection and emphasis and (if small enough) through convenience. Which is one of the aims of this effort. Below, you will find a list of those which helped shape *Mending Scotland's* argument. It draws on earlier writings of my own, in particular *The Rise and Fall of Regional Europe* (London: Routledge, 1993); and *Fool's Gold: the Story of North Sea Oil* (London: Penguin, 1994).

Books consulted while writing include:
Antony, Jay *Corporation Man* London: Penguin, 1975
Ascherson, Neal *Stone Voices* London: Granta, 2002
Borja, Jordi and Castells, Manuel *Local & Global: Management of Cities in the Information Age* London: Earthscan Publications Limited, 1997
Bort, Eberhard and Evans, Neil *Networking Europe: Essays in Regionalism and Social Democracy* Liverpool: Liverpool University Press, 2000
Brady, Ciaran ed *Interpreting Irish History: the Debate on Historical Revisionism* Dublin: Irish Acad. Press, 1994
Brown, Gordon *Where There Is Greed* Edinburgh: Mainstream, 1989

Colley, Linda *Britons: Forging the Nation* London: Yale
    University Press, 1992

Craig, Carol *The Scots' Crisis of Confidence* Edinburgh: Big
    Thinking, 2003

Crouch, Colin *Coping with Post-Democracy* London: Fabian
    Society, 2001

Curtice, John, et al., eds *New Scotland, New Society? Are Social
    and Political Ties Fragmenting?* Edinburgh: Polygon, 2002

Davies, Norman *The Isles* London: Macmillan, 1999

Devine, Tom, ed *Being Scots* Edinburgh: Edin Univ Press, 2003

Emmot, Bill *20/21 Vision* London: Penguin, 2002

Enzenberger, Hans-Magnus *Europe! Europe!* London: Radius, 1989

Finlay, Richard *Modern Scotland 1914-2000* London: Profile
    Books, 2004

Foster, John et al. *Paying the Piper: Capital and Labour in the
    Offshore Oil Industry* London: Macmillan, 1996

Garitaonondia, Carmelo 'European Regional Television ' in
    Television: Critical Concepts London: Routledge, 2003

Hassan, Gerry and Warhurst, Chris, eds *: A Different Future: A
    Modernisers' Guide to Scotland* Glasgow: Centre for Scottish
    Public Policy and The Big Issue in Scotland, 1999

Hassan, Gerry ed *The Scottish Labour Party: History, Institutions
    and Ideas* Edinburgh: Edinburgh University Press, 2004

Hutton, Will *The State to Come* London: Vintage, 1997

Hutton, Will *The State We're In* London: Vintage, 1993

Jack, Ian *The Crash that Stopped* Britain London: Granta, 2001

Jamieson, Bill ed *An Illustrated Guide to the Scottish Economy*
    London: Duckworth, 1999

Lee, Clive *Scotland in the United Kingdom*, Manchester:
    Manchester University Press, 1995

Lee, Joseph *Ireland, 1912-1985* Cambridge: Cambridge
    University Press, 1990

McCormick, James and Leicester, Graham *Three Nations:
    Social Exclusion in Scotland* Edinburgh: Scottish
    Council Foundation, 1998

McCrone, David *Understanding Scotland: the Sociology of a
    Nation London*: Routledge, 2001

Marquand, David *The Unprincipled Society: New Demands and old Politics* Glasgow: Fontana Press, 1988

Mulgan, Geoff ed *Life after Politics: New Thinking for the twenty-first Century* London: Fontana Press, 1997

Nairn, Tom *After Britain: New Labour and the Return of Scotland*, London: Granta, 2000

Nairn, Tom *Faces of Nationalism* London: Verso, 1997

OECD *Devolution and Globalisation: Implications for local Decision-Makers* Paris: OECD Publications, 2001

O'Hagan, Andrew *The Death of British Farming* London: LRB, 2001

Paterson, Lindsay, et al., *New Scotland, New Politics?* Edinburgh: Polygon, 2001

Rawnsley, Andrew *Servants of the People: The inside Story of New Labour* London: Penguin, 2001

Rifkin, Jeremy *Age of Access* London: Penguin, 2000

Scottish Affairs No. 1, 1993 to No. 47, 2004

Scottish Executive *National planning Framework for Scotland* Edinburgh: Astron, 2004

Sheridan, Tommy and McCombes, Alan *Imagine: A Socialist Vision for the 21st Century* Edinburgh: Rebel Inc., 2000

Statistisches Landesamt Baden-Württemberg ed *Statistisches Taschenbuch 2003* Stuttgart: Statistisches Landesamt Baden-Württemberg, 2003

Taylor, Brian *Scotland's Parliament: Triumph and Disaster* Edinburgh: Edinburgh University Press, 2002

The Economist: The World in 2004 London: Economist, 2003

Todd, Emanuel *The Causes of Progress: Culture, Authority and Change* Oxford: Blackwell, 1989

Trench, Alan and Hazell, Robert, ed *The State of the Nations 2000-2004* (4 Vols) London and Exeter: Constitution Unit and Imprint Academic, 2004

Wagner, Adolf *Regionalentwicklung in Baden-Württemberg* Tübingen: Francke, 1994

Weight, Richard *Patriots: National Identity in Britain 1840-2000* London: Macmillan, 2002

Acknowledgements

Parts of I.i appeared in *The London Review of Books* and *Scotland on Sunday* (2002); I.ii in *Scottish Affairs* and *Scottish Studies Review* (2000); a more extended version of II.iv appeared in *The Drouth* (summer 2004), II.iii in the *Guardian* (2004). II.v owes much to 'The Moral Sense of Inspector Rebus' in *Scotland in Theory*, ed. Eleanor Bell and Gavin Miller (Rodopi, 2004); III.i. was given as a talk to European diplomats arranged by the SNP Brussels branch on 20 March 2003 (the day the Iraq war broke out!) and an abridged version came out in the Institute of Welsh Affairs's *Agenda*, summer 2004. III.ii was delivered to the Salford Media Conference on December 2003 and III.iii appeared in 2001 in the *Times Educational Supplement, Scotland*. III.iv first appeared in *The Scotsman*.

I am grateful for permission to reprint to the editors concerned, and to Paul Laity, Valentina Bold, Lindsay Paterson, Eberhard Bort, Seumas Milne, Johnny Rodger, Eleanor Bell and Gavin Miller, John Osmond, Sandy Ross, Neil Munro and George Kerevan. Besides whom, thanks to Lawrence Marshall, Richard Finlay, Faith Liddell, Douglas MacLeod, Mike Russell, Mark Lazarowicz MP, Lord Steel, Manfred Hattendorf, Richard Wyn Jones and the WiRE group, and my family in Scotland and Germany.

Index

AFORE YE GO. . .

- Before World War I, Clydeside engineering magnates wanted to use 'scientific management' to break down the work of their fearsome skilled men into simplified tasks that could, according to the guru F W Taylor 'be performed by trained gorillas'. Not only did the workers revolt, but managers were over-stressed by chopping up jobs and having to reassemble them, failed to communicate with a distrustful workforce. The big idea had to be given up. Remind you of anyone, Bank of Scotland directors?

- Henry Ford once jested to one of his assembly-line workers: 'The next machine I have in mind will get rid of your job, too.' And the worker said, 'So who's going to buy your cars?'

- These old stories come to mind as I watch the Scottish economy cough and splutter. Gordon Brown is paid circa £150,000 to guide it; Sir Fred Goodwin perhaps twenty times that to enrich the shareholders of the Royal Bank. And beneath both is a workforce whose welfare and experience isn't growing at all, increasingly regarded as a dispensable 'human resource'. But are the folk who build the rigs and equip the factories, who navigate their trains and lorries through our crumbling infrastructure, who try to instil reason and values in kids who are otherwise fair game for rapacious retailers, not worth consulting on their own economy?

- Scotland is where the new lottery of inequality has really started to hurt – not just the ever-more-insecure employee, or the unpaid carer, but the would-be-entrepreneur, whose talents are no less remarkable than those of the megabanker or the Westminster matador. The latter are beginning to be seen as standing in the way of the acquisition of new technologies – to prolong the life of the oilfields, to make Scotland Europe's break-bulk port, to weld our cities into a true conurbation. Tom Johnston said 'that which men do together, they *can* do.' In this, are our masters with us? And if they are not, should they be our masters at all?